Monitoring with Opsview

Leverage the power of Opsview to effectively monitor your physical, virtual, and private cloud infrastructure

Alan Wijntje

BIRMINGHAM - MUMBAI

Monitoring with Opsview

Copyright © 2013 Packt Publishing

First published: December 2013

Production Reference: 1061213

Published by Packt Publishing Ltd.
Livery Place
35 Livery Street
Birmingham B3 2PB, UK.

ISBN 978-1-78328-473-3

www.packtpub.com

Cover Image by Benoit Benedetti (benoit.benedetti@gmail.com)

Credits

Author
Alan Wijntje

Reviewers
Duncan Ferguson
Jesse A. Griffin
Surendra Mohan

Acquisition Editor
Rubal Kaur

Commissioning Editor
Mohammed Fahad

Technical Editors
Rahul U. Nair
Anita Nayak
Rohit Kumar Singh

Project Coordinator
Sageer Parkar

Proofreader
Maria Gould

Copy Editors
Alisha Aranha
Roshni Banerjee
Gladson Monteiro
Deepa Nambiar
Karuna Narayanan
Kirti Pai
Laxmi Subramanian

Indexer
Rekha Nair

Production Coordinator
Saiprasad Kadam

Cover Work
Saiprasad Kadam

About the Author

Alan Wijntje has been working in the IT field since 2000 when he started out as a simple technician providing local IT support to various companies.

Figuring out why something broke (and then fixing it) soon became his specialty, and he outgrew this job within a couple of years; his employer was quick to recognize this, and within days, he was given a new assignment to work on the NOC for a major Dutch ISP.

After settling in, Alan quickly started to get to grips with the various monitoring systems and was soon making various improvements.

His love for Linux was a great asset when he was granted more and more freedom to tinker with various systems, including Netcool OMNIbus and Nagios.

After three years (and a company merger), Alan moved to another department that was solely responsible for all monitoring systems (most notable were Netcool OMNIbus and Nagios), and he was put in charge of all Nagios-based systems.

Running a lot of separate Nagios systems was, however, a lot of work and soon plans were made to move to a more user-friendly, flexible, and scalable solution.

Opsview was introduced as the replacement, and the system was built in record time after which Alan spent most of his time writing new plugins, fixing plugins, thinking up new ways of tackling various monitoring requirements (such as using Selenium for web-based tests), and so on.

After about three years of being the Opsview administrator, Alan again moved his department to join one of the networking teams (his other passion) where he got to play around with data center switches, virtual switches, and firewalls.

Although, technically, he is no longer an Opsview administrator, he still loves to help out (sometimes a bit too much some would say), write plugins, and even spend lots of time on the Opsview forum and the #opsview IRC channel helping others out.

Alan has worked for the Dutch company, QNH, since he started in IT, and over the years, they have always been quick to recognize his interests and talents and have helped him develop these skills (even some he never knew he had).

Acknowledgments

Now I'm sure I'll forget to thank someone when I finish this, so I apologize for this beforehand.

I do know for sure I need to thank my girlfriend Karin, my family, and friends (especially Jurriaan for being my "nerd buddy") for letting me off the hook whenever I had to cancel or postpone dates while writing this book.

A very big thank-you to the guys at Opsview and a special thank-you to Duncan, Neil, Ton, Rob, and Adnan for all their help and support over the years that I have been running/using/playing around with Opsview (and for listening to me whenever I have some weird and wild feature request or idea).

Of course the guys in my old monitoring team: Arjan, Frans, Job, and Robin for letting me build and be in charge of the Opsview environment and helping me out whenever I needed support.

A special thank-you must also go to Duncan, Jesse, and Surendra, who reviewed this book and did a fantastic job by keeping me on my toes and providing essential feedback and recommendations.

And last but not the least I would like to thank the people at QNH and specially my manager Ruud and our Qniversity manager Diana for supporting me on this endeavor and for always helping me out with whatever I needed.

About the Reviewers

Duncan Ferguson works at Opsview Limited and has been working with Opsview since early 2007. In this time, he has worked on feature design, development, and provided consultancy for the product. He is currently the Support Team Leader and acts as the third-line support for all issues, although he still acts in other capacities as required, including diving into the code to fix problems.

He looks after a number of freeware projects and Perl modules as well as authoring and maintaining ClusterSSH, a popular administration tool.

In what remains of his spare time, Duncan is a devoted father, husband, animal carer, scuba diver, and skier, although not all at the same time.

Jesse A. Griffin is a system administrator with experience in Linux, FreeBSD, and Windows. Day-to-day, he designs, implements, and maintains clusters, databases, e-mail systems, highly available storage, monitoring systems, websites, and performs all types of open source administration tasks for clients around the world.

When not working, he teaches Old Testament and the Hebrew language at his church. He also provides consulting services for several nonprofit and educational institutions.

> I would like to thank tummy.com, ltd. for allowing me the time to review this book.

Surendra Mohan is currently serving as Drupal Consultant-cum-Drupal Architect at a well-known software consulting organization in India. Prior to joining this organization, he served a few Indian MNCs and a couple of startups in varied roles, such as Programmer, Technical Lead, Project Lead, Project Manager, Solution Architect, and Service Delivery Manager. He has around nine years of working experience in web technologies covering media and entertainment, real estate, travel and tours, publishing, e-learning, enterprise architecture, and so on. He is also a speaker-cum-trainer who delivers talks on Drupal, Open Source, PHP, Moodle, and so on, along with organizing and delivering TechTalks in Drupal meetups and Drupal Camps in Mumbai, India.

He also runs his blog at `http://www.surendramohan.info/`, mainly discussing hot, new, and upcoming technical topics. Moreover, he is the author of the book *Administrating Solr*, published by Packt Publishing.

He has also reviewed other technical books, such as *Drupal 7 Multi-site Configuration* and *Drupal Search Engine Optimization*, titles on Drupal commerce, ElasticSearch, Drupal-related video tutorials, and many more.

I would like to thank my family and friends who supported and encouraged me in completing my reviews on time to a high quality.

www.PacktPub.com

Support files, eBooks, discount offers and more

You might want to visit www.PacktPub.com for support files and downloads related to your book.

Did you know that Packt offers eBook versions of every book published, with PDF and ePub files available? You can upgrade to the eBook version at www.PacktPub.com and as a print book customer, you are entitled to a discount on the eBook copy. Get in touch with us at service@packtpub.com for more details.

At www.PacktPub.com, you can also read a collection of free technical articles, sign up for a range of free newsletters and receive exclusive discounts and offers on Packt books and eBooks.

http://PacktLib.PacktPub.com

Do you need instant solutions to your IT questions? PacktLib is Packt's online digital book library. Here, you can access, read and search across Packt's entire library of books.

Why Subscribe?

- Fully searchable across every book published by Packt
- Copy and paste, print and bookmark content
- On demand and accessible via web browser

Free Access for Packt account holders

If you have an account with Packt at www.PacktPub.com, you can use this to access PacktLib today and view nine entirely free books. Simply use your login credentials for immediate access.

Table of Contents

Preface

In today's IT world, staying on top of your environment is important but also very complex.

With the introduction of cloud-based applications and services, having a grip on your IT estate becomes paramount, no matter where it resides and who operates it.

The Opsview monitoring system allows you to keep track of your IT environment by creating a single pane of view in your entire IT estate.

What this book covers

Chapter 1, *Opsview Core Basics*, introduces Opsview Core concepts and how to get started with it.

Chapter 2, *Basic Configuration*, deals with adding hosts in a fast and easy way using some of the unique features of Opsview.

Chapter 3, *Advanced Configuration*, deals with using some exciting Opsview features to create flexible views of your IT estate, automation, and much more advanced features.

Chapter 4, *Agents, Clouds, and Modules*, deals with Agent or Agentless monitoring and monitoring of cloud services and virtual environments, including a look at the Opsview Core modules.

Chapter 5, *Opsview Mobile*, explains how anytime and anywhere access to your Opsview monitoring system is possible using mobile applications.

Chapter 6, *The Three Ts*, deals with the debugging and testing of new plugins, understanding common plugin issues, and using the special command-line tools that come with Opsview Core.

Chapter 7, Designing a Monitoring Environment, deals with designing a monitoring setup that will support you in your needs and requirements, along with some considerations to ponder.

Chapter 8, Upgrading to Opsview Pro or Opsview Enterprise, deals with upgrading your Opsview installation to a fully-supported and even more feature-rich Opsview release.

Chapter 9, Opsview Pro Features, teaches us how to use the advanced modules that come with Opsview Pro, such as auto discovery for rapid deployments.

Chapter 10, Opsview Enterprise Features, explains the distributed monitoring of large IT environments and other modules that come with Opsview Enterprise.

Chapter 11, Additional Modules, teaches how to extend your Opsview installation with NetFlow, NetAudit, and the multi-master module.

Chapter 12, Opsview Dashboards, deals with dashboards, which you can visualize anything you monitor and make your monitoring come to life with eye-catching dashboards.

What you need for this book

It is strongly suggested that you have a system ready where you can install Opsview and where you can try out anything mentioned in the book.

Who this book is for

This book is aimed at monitoring networks, from small IT environments to large distributed environments located all over the world.

Technical and non-technical stakeholders in IT environments looking for a new and better way of keeping track of their environment will also benefit from the book.

Conventions

In this book, you will find a number of styles of text that distinguish between different kinds of information. Here are some examples of these styles, and an explanation of their meaning.

Code words in text, database table names, folder names, filenames, file extensions, pathnames, dummy URLs, user input, and Twitter handles are shown as follows: "You can change this by logging in to the server with SSH using both username and password as `conf` and running the NETCONF utility."

Any command-line input or output is written as follows:

```
check_mysql -H $HOSTADDRESS$ -u myhrmuser -p myhrmpassword -d HRM
```

New terms and **important words** are shown in bold. Words that you see on the screen, in menus or dialog boxes for example, appear in the text like this: "When creating a new SNMP service, enter the name of your host in the **Example Host** field and click on **SNMP Walk** to scan the host."

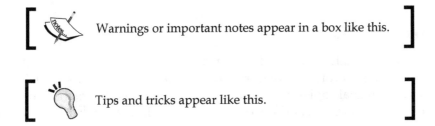

> Warnings or important notes appear in a box like this.

> Tips and tricks appear like this.

Reader feedback

Feedback from our readers is always welcome. Let us know what you think about this book—what you liked or may have disliked. Reader feedback is important for us to develop titles that you really get the most out of.

To send us general feedback, simply send an e-mail to feedback@packtpub.com, and mention the book title via the subject of your message.

If there is a topic that you have expertise in and you are interested in either writing or contributing to a book, see our author guide on www.packtpub.com/authors.

Customer support

Now that you are the proud owner of a Packt book, we have a number of things to help you to get the most from your purchase.

Errata

Although we have taken every care to ensure the accuracy of our content, mistakes do happen. If you find a mistake in one of our books—maybe a mistake in the text or the code—we would be grateful if you would report this to us. By doing so, you can save other readers from frustration and help us improve subsequent versions of this book. If you find any errata, please report them by visiting http://www.packtpub.com/submit-errata, selecting your book, clicking on the **errata submission form** link, and entering the details of your errata. Once your errata are verified, your submission will be accepted and the errata will be uploaded on our website, or added to any list of existing errata, under the Errata section of that title. Any existing errata can be viewed by selecting your title from http://www.packtpub.com/support.

Piracy

Piracy of copyright material on the Internet is an ongoing problem across all media. At Packt, we take the protection of our copyright and licenses very seriously. If you come across any illegal copies of our works, in any form, on the Internet, please provide us with the location address or website name immediately so that we can pursue a remedy.

Please contact us at copyright@packtpub.com with a link to the suspected pirated material.

We appreciate your help in protecting our authors, and our ability to bring you valuable content.

Questions

You can contact us at questions@packtpub.com if you are having a problem with any aspect of the book, and we will do our best to address it.

1
Opsview Core Basics

Having a monitoring system that works well has become one of the most important prerequisites of any modern IT environment, and with operations expanding and changing quickly, we need a monitoring system that is as flexible and adaptive as possible.

In times where we are seeing companies move to the cloud or using a more service-based environment, effectively monitoring all these various systems is of paramount importance.

In this chapter we will look into some of the concepts behind Opsview and how to install and get started using the various tools provided by Opsview to help us deploy a simple monitoring solution.

Important concepts

Opsview offers an easy to use, highly configurable, and robust monitoring platform, providing IT departments with a unique view into the health of their IT estate.

For those already well versed with the world of monitoring, there are some conceptual differences in how Opsview approaches monitoring in comparison to other solutions (if you are new to the subject, please read on as these concepts will help you understand how Opsview operates).

If you are new to the subject, have a look at the official documentation site for Opsview (`http://docs.opsview.com`) and the blogs from Opsview (`http://www.opsview.com/whats-new`).

At its core, Opsview aims to be a single window for your IT operations, giving a centralized, multi-layered view into the heart of your environment and offering a variety of ways to keep it healthy and operating at peak efficiency.

Flexibility is the key part of a system and using smart and adaptive methods allows for a versatile setup, and seemingly complex monitoring challenges can be easily configured and maintained.

Information gathered by Opsview can be viewed in various different forms and depending on what type of data we are looking at, using these different forms can help you better understand and interpret vital information related to your IT operations.

While in most cases being flexible means there are too many options to configure, Opsview aims at being easy to use and easy to configure by using templates, cloning, and automation to vastly simplify running and maintaining a system. Opsview uses the powerful **Nagios** engine at its core, performing various tasks when users interact with the Opsview web interface (`http://your-opsview-system:3000`) to handle all the configuration and display tasks.

Installing and configuring Opsview Core

Getting your first Opsview system running is actually relatively easy as Opsview offers three different ways of getting started:

- Packages
- Virtual appliance
- On demand

Depending on your requirements you can choose the installation type that suits you best.

Please note that the username/password or even installation instructions might change, so check out the Opsview documentation website for the latest instructions and the Opsview download page (`http://www.opsview.com/technology/downloads/opsview-core`).

Package-based installations

Opsview provides packages for the most common Linux distributions, and if you are already running any of these packages, installing them becomes very easy indeed.

The Linux distributions supported are:

- Red Hat Enterprise Linux
- Ubuntu (LTS releases)
- Debian

- SUSE Linux Enterprise
- CentOS

For the most up-to-date list of supported systems, visit `http://docs.opsview.com/doku.php?id=opsview-core:platforms`.

Prerequisites

Depending on your operating system, you may need to take some additional steps to address the few prerequisites that Opsview has:

- **Security-Enhanced Linux extensions (SELinux)**: Currently, Opsview is not compatible with SELinux, so if SELinux is enabled on your system, you have to disable it.

- **CentOS**: On CentOS systems, **RPMForge** must be set up to resolve any dependencies Opsview may have, so make sure it is enabled (visit `http://repoforge.org` for the latest version).

- **Red Hat Enterprise Linux**: On Red Hat EL 6, the **Red Hat Optional Server 6** repositories must be enabled in RHN (Red Hat Network).

  Both EL 5 and EL 6 systems need to have a recent version of libmcrypt installed, which can be downloaded at `http://dl.fedoraproject.org/pub/epel/<version>/x86_64`. Check the repository for the latest version, and enter it in the URL. For example, the URL `http://dl.fedoraproject.org/pub/epel/6/x86_64` is for RHEL 6.

- **Debian/Ubuntu**: The Opsview repositories for Debian and Ubuntu are GPG-signed (where GPG stands for GNU Privacy Guard) for security. To prevent issues with **APT (Advanced Packaging Tool)** not being able to verify the contents of the repository, enter the following in the command line:

  ```
  sudo gpg --keyserver subkeys.pgp.net --recv-key 0FC6984B
  sudo gpg --export --armor 0FC6984B | sudo apt-key add -
  ```

  This will install the APT key for Opsview (on occasions, retrieving the key fails due to an unresponsive pgp.net server; simply wait for a couple of minutes and try again).

- **SUSE Linux Enterprise**: To resolve all dependencies make sure the **Extras** repo is enabled on your system. For this we type the following command:

  ```
  zypper mr -e nu_novell_com:SLES11-Extras
  ```

Installing Opsview

Once all the prerequisites are met you can add the repositories, and install Opsview using your favorite package manager.

From the Opsview download page, select the distribution you would like to install as shown in the following screenshot, and you will be redirected to the latest install guides:

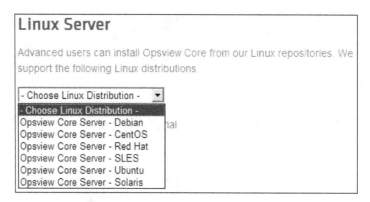

Virtual appliance

Opsview also offers a virtual appliance version of Opsview Core that can be installed into ESX, vSphere, or VMware Player environments.

Download the virtual appliance from the Opsview download page as shown in the following screenshot:

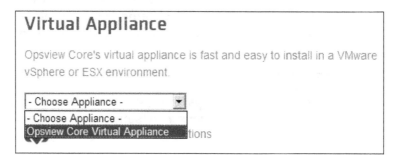

Deploy it and power up the Virtual Machine (VM).

By default, VM is configured to use **DHCP (Dynamic Host Configuration Protocol)** for an IP address which might be undesirable (the current IP is displayed on the console when the server is running).

You can change this by logging into the server with **SSH (Secure Shell)** using both the username and password as conf and running the NETCONF utility.

On demand

The last of the three possible installation methods of Opsview Core is the on-demand version that runs in Amazon EC2.

Running Opsview Core is free of charge, but the EC2 instance will be charged by Amazon.

Opsview Core running on the recommended m1.small general purpose type should be able to monitor up to 250 hosts (the number might vary depending on the number of checks, frequency, and so on).

To install, first make sure you have a working AWS account, then select the datacenter closest to you from the Opsview website, and within seconds you can have a running instance of Opsview Core by simply following the instructions. The selection list is shown in the following screenshot:

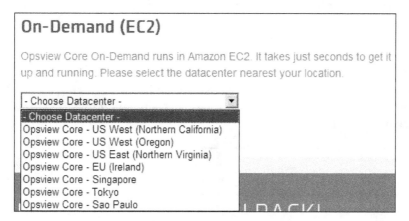

Using the Opsview help system and contextual menus

Now that we have our Opsview installation up and running, it's time to log in (http://your-opsview-system:3000) with the default username (admin) and password (initial).

During the course of this book, we will be looking at a lot of different items in Opsview. So keep an Opsview system close at hand to try out the various items we will be covering.

The first page we see once we log in is the main status screen, which at the moment will show only the Opsview host group. Simply drill down into the group to get more information about your Opsview system. At the top of the screen we have various menus we can open to perform various tasks in Opsview.

The first very important feature of Opsview is the **help system**, which we can use while configuring various items; the second is the **contextual menu**.

To see both in action, go to the **settings** menu (as shown in the following screenshot) and click on **hosts** in the **Basic** column.

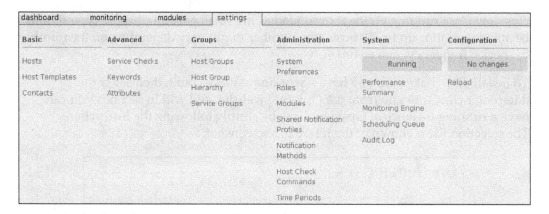

This will bring up the host list. The host list shown in the following screenshot shows you all the hosts currently in Opsview. As it has been newly installed, only the default Opsview host is listed.

Contextual menu

If you look carefully at the host list, you will see a small arrow just after the Opsview icon. This small arrow is the contextual menu and it will appear on various pages and have various functions depending on the page you are looking at.

Have a go at checking the contextual menu in different pages under the **monitoring** menu, before returning to the host list.

Opsview help system

Now let's go back to the host list and select the Opsview host by clicking on the name.

By doing this we will enter the edit page for the host and you will see the various fields and tabs that are used to define a host. A small portion of the first screen is shown in the following screenshot:

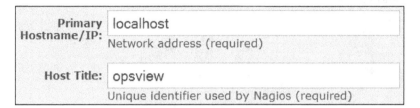

Each field is preceded by a short text describing the field. Clicking on any of the descriptions will redirect you to a help page explaining the field and any restrictions it might have. This is the Opsview help system, and is available within all the pages in the **settings** menu.

Creating user accounts

Now that we have a running Opsview installation, it is time to look at user management.

Within Opsview, a user is referred to as a **contact** while the group he or she belongs to is called a **role**.

Permissions and views (what a contact can see in Opsview) are based on the role a contact belongs to. The Opsview help system is available within these screens, and so we'll only cover the most important parts just to get you going (I strongly advise you to play around with various settings to get a feel for the permissions).

Adding and assigning roles

Creating roles is done by going to **settings** | **Administration** | **Roles**.

You can either add a new role by clicking on the green plus sign (located at the upper-left corner of the screen), or use the clone function to copy an existing set (removing a role can be achieved by clicking on the trash bin icon). The following screenshot shows the three icons add, delete, and clone:

 Clone and delete are available in all configuration pages, allowing you to quickly add or remove items.

During the installation a number of predefined roles were created; the names reflect the type of access they provide.

Select any of the predefined roles to bring up the edit screen. Each role has been split into a number of subsections, each responsible for specific parts of the system, as shown in the following screenshot:

Of these, **Status Access**, **Status Objects**, and **Configuration** are the three most important roles, as they define which parts of Opsview the contact can view (**Status Access**), which objects the contact can see (**Status Objects**), and which parts the contact can configure (**Configuration**).

Depending on your organizational needs, we can use these permissions to create various types of roles.

Just to illustrate how powerful this is, imagine we have a single system running an OS, a web server, and a database. Each is maintained by different groups (system admins, web admins, and database admins). Using the correct **Status Objects** and **Status Access** settings, we can make sure each group only sees the information relevant to its role (so database admins only see information related to the databases, web admins only see information related to the web server, and so on).

When we apply this to the **Configuration** settings, we can even allow our database admins to make changes within this host, while the web admins might not perform such actions.

As each organization is unique in its needs, try to create a role setup that reflects these needs.

Adding contacts

Once we have finished creating the various roles we need, it's time to add some contacts to our system by navigating to **settings | Basic | Contacts**, to go to the contacts list.

Creating contacts is a fairly straightforward task, simply click on the add or clone button and enter the requested information as shown in the following screenshot (**Name**, **Username**, and so on), and select the role the user belongs to.

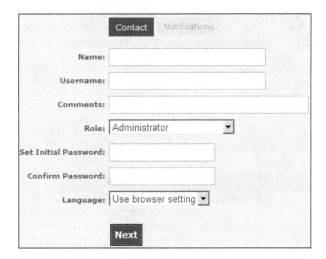

Click on **Next** to create the contact and go to the **Notifications** screen from where we can finalize the contact; if you are planning on using e-mails to alert contacts, you can add the e-mail address as well.

LDAP and Active Directory integration

Instead of creating contacts manually, it is possible to integrate Opsview with your **Active Directory (AD)** or your **Lightweight Directory Access Protocol (LDAP)** server. This allows you to either authenticate against LDAP (you will need to create the contacts), or automatically create, delete, and update contacts within Opsview based on your LDAP.

You can get more information on LDAP integration at `http://docs.opsview.com/doku.php?id=opsview-core:ldap`.

Reloading

Any configuration changes made will not go into effect until Opsview has performed a reload. You can see the changes that have not yet taken place in the **settings** menu as shown in the following screenshot:

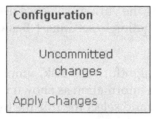

Click on **settings** | **Configuration** | **Apply Changes** and from the **Status and Reload** screen, click on **Reload Configuration** to apply any changes.

Summary

In this chapter we have covered quite a bit of ground.

We looked at the main concepts of Opsview and the various ways of installing Opsview, and made some headway in getting your Opsview system ready for business.

In the next chapter we will look into configuring hosts, creating service checks, and even introduce you to some new special features included in Opsview.

2

Basic Configuration

Now that we have the Opsview installation running and have seen how to manage user access, it is time to look into the basics of monitoring using Opsview.

We will look at how we can add hosts, new functionality (plugins), and manage these various parts in an easy way.

Those familiar with **Nagios** will recognize a lot of terms and definitions but will also see some new ones that are specific to Opsview.

Configuring hosts, host groups, and host group hierarchy

As most organizations are divided into departments, IT systems are commonly divided into various groups depending on their function. Opsview allows a similar segregation into various groups, which are used by the roles to grant access or configure privileges.

[Remember, the Opsview help system is available in all configuration-related screens.]

Host groups

As the name suggests, a host group is nothing more than a container that holds various hosts. This makes it possible to have all your database systems visible as status objects from one view, or to have multiple database host groups depending on the type of database. Base your host groups on what your organization needs.

Host groups can be created by going to **settings | Groups | Host Groups**.

The following screenshot shows the default host group of **Monitoring Servers**, which contains the Opsview host:

So let's create our own host group by clicking on the add icon (as shown in *Chapter 1, Opsview Core Basics*), then enter a name (test group 1 for instance), and submit the changes. Repeat this to create a couple of host groups (we will use them later on). We should now see two (or more) host groups, one containing the Opsview host and the other containing no hosts.

 You can drag-and-drop hosts from one group to another in this view.

Deleting host groups is possible only when it contains no hosts; if you wish to remove a host group, first move all the hosts to another group. Try to keep the naming of your host groups logical so that others can easily navigate through the various groups.

Host group hierarchy

Once we have created a couple of host groups, we might want to group some of them together to create a tree-based view or a hierarchical view. Using the host group hierarchy, we can add host groups with similar systems together, or even group them based on departments, or order by relevance.

For this, we use the host group hierarchy view by going to **settings | Groups | Host Group**.

 We can use the contextual menu here to make changes such as adding a new child group (which will create an empty host group).

We can also use this view to move host groups from one group to another by simply dragging-and-dropping them. If you have made the test groups, try moving them around.

 You cannot move a host group into another host group if the destination host group contains hosts (a host group can only contain hosts or other host groups but not both).

Setting up a good structure for your host groups is very important. So, make sure to fit it to your organization's needs as it will make traversing the host group view, under **monitoring | Status Summary | Host Groups**, a lot easier.

A good structure will also help in setting up your roles (status objects) making sure everyone sees the information they need to access (or need to be able to configure).

Shown here is an example of a host group hierarchy divided into smaller groups depending on the application or database, with databases split into MySQL and Oracle, applications split into Finance or HR, and so on.

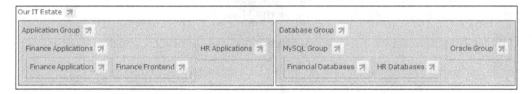

Hosts

Now that we have a basic layout of host groups and our hierarchy, it is time to add our hosts to the system. For this, we go to **settings | Basic | Hosts**. The screen will currently have only the Opsview host defined. Just add a host by clicking on the add icon or by cloning. Cloning is a great way of adding similar hosts in a fast and efficient way.

When we add a new host, there are some options we can fill out or choose from. For now, we will stick to the defaults for most values and focus on the most important parts (but do take some time to look at the various options available on this screen).

The following screenshot shows a small portion of the **New Host** page:

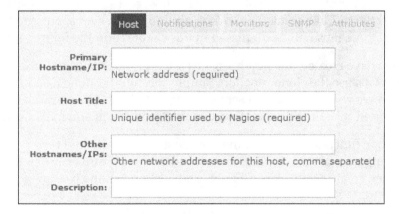

There are two **required** fields in the host screen, **Primary Hostname / IP**
(which is either an IP address or a Fully Qualified Domain Name)
and **Host Title** (which is how the host will be displayed within Opsview).

There is a very important distinction between the two fields and how
they are applied within service checks and within Opsview in terms of
information management.

Imagine that we have a host named hostX with **Primary Hostname** as hostx.
example.com, but we need to migrate it to hostx.second.example.com. By
simply changing the primary hostname, all the data collected for hostX is
preserved (all the data is collected under the **Host Title**).

Now let's create a test host so we can see the process involved in adding a new host.

Set the primary hostname and input a host title, select an appropriate host group
(and icon if you want) and click on **Next**, which will take us to the notification screen,
as shown in the following screenshot:

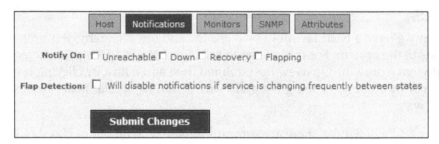

Select any settings you want, after which we can Submit our changes and then we
will have added a new host to our system.

There are a number of tabs available within the host edit screen, each responsible
for various settings. Take some time to look around in these tabs, but don't worry
though as all these tabs will be discussed in this chapter and the following chapter.

Now that we have created our first host, let's make another one; but instead of using
the add icon let's use the clone function. Simply click on the clone icon in front of our
first host and we will go to the edit screen of our new host. Make any adjustments
that are required (like host title) and needed (like primary hostname) and submit.

Using the clone function makes adding new hosts a lot easier and faster. So, when
you are adding new hosts in Opsview, always look for a similar host already there,
or maybe even create some example hosts that contain just the basics.

Host templates

While adding the host, you might have noticed the host template section at the bottom of the edit screen. Much like a host group is a group of hosts, a host template is a set of service checks grouped together for a specific purpose.

By default, Opsview comes with a vast amount of readymade templates containing checks for the most common applications. To find out what a template does, select it from the right-hand side column and click on **Template details**.

You can create your own templates by going to **settings | Basic | Host Templates** and clicking on the add icon.

As shown in the following screenshot, our new host template contains a number of tabs:

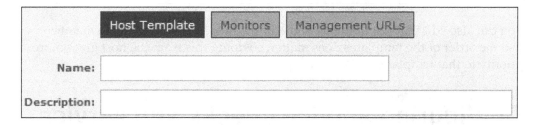

Enter the name of your template and a clear description of its intended purpose in the **Host Template** tab.

From the **Monitors** tab, which we have in the host edit screen too, you can select any service check that you wish to include in the template. Service checks are grouped by service group, both of which we will discuss soon.

In the **Management URL** section, you can add references to online documentation or internal wikis. These URLs will then be made available in the contextual menu when the host is viewed in the monitoring view.

You can use multiple host templates within a single host, where any duplicate settings (or service checks) in the template are handled based on the order in which the templates are applied, with the first template taking precedence.

Any check directly assigned to a host, through the **Monitors** tab in the host edit screen, will take precedence over any duplicate checks assigned through a host template. To assign a template to a host, simply edit the host, select the template, and click on the arrow pointing to the left. You can use the up and down arrows to reorder your templates. The Opsview host with multiple templates assigned is shown here:

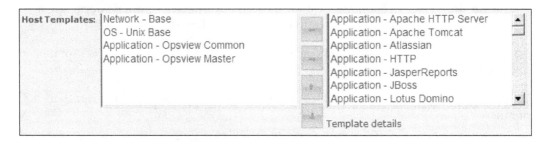

You can also edit the host template and add the host to the template. Remember that the order of the templates does matter, so doing this from the host gives more priority to that template.

Configuring service checks and service groups

Now that we have seen how to add hosts and create and assign host templates, we need to look at the service checks that will actually perform the checks we need.

Creating service checks

To create a service check (or edit or clone an existing one), simply go to **settings | Advanced | Service Checks** and you will get a list of all the available checks.

Let's create a new check by clicking on the add icon, which will open the **New Service Check** page as shown in the following screenshot:

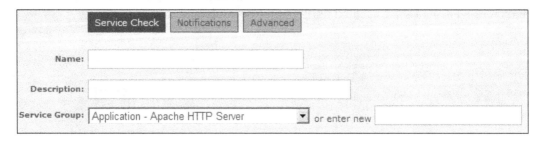

After naming and describing the check, the **Service Group** field is the most important one to look at. You can either select one that is already defined or create a new one. Note that the service group is used only within the host template's **monitors** tab for ordering and finding the checks easily.

The next important selection is the type of check (similar to Nagios). The following screenshot shows the three basic types of checks from which we can choose:

The type simply tells Opsview how it is supposed to operate the check by either executing it (**Active Plugin**), or by waiting for another program to send in its status (**Passive**).

SNMP Polling is a special type that allows you to create SNMP-based service checks in a fast and easy manner.

Active Plugin

When we select **Active Plugin**, we need to select a plugin from the **Plugin** dropdown and possibly add the arguments to be used (in the **Arguments** field) by the plugin on execution.

The following screenshot shows the **Plugin** and **Arguments** section of the **New Service Check** screen.

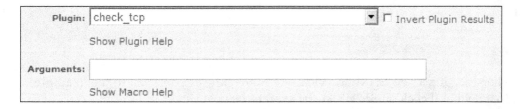

To understand what a plugin does, simply select the plugin you want from the drop-down menu and click on **Show Plugin Help** to display the help page.

Most plugins use the arguments given by the user in the **Arguments** field to give the specific information you want to retrieve and the thresholds it should apply to the results.

As Opsview uses Nagios as its engine, it allows the use of macros to make configurations more generic. One of the most common macros is $HOSTADDRESS$, which represents the host's primary hostname / IP (we discussed this in the *Hosts* section). Click on **Show Macro Help** to get a list of available macros.

SNMP polling

For those familiar with SNMP, using it to retrieve information can be a challenge as you would need to know the exact **Object Identifier** (OID) to be retrieved.

Opsview allows you to easily create SNMP checks by letting you scan an example host and returning all possible OIDs ready for use.

To use this feature, you will first need to configure your host to allow SNMP from the Opsview system. Then you need to configure SNMP in the host configuration. Test the connection using **Test SNMP connection**.

The following screenshot is an example of a host that is configured to use SNMP with the community set to public and after the **Test SNMP connection** option was run successfully:

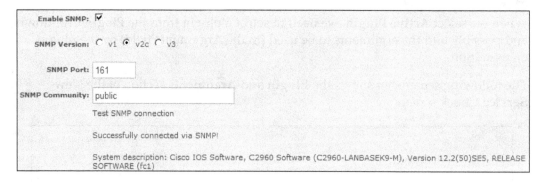

When creating a new SNMP service, enter the name of your host in the **Example Host** field and click on **SNMP Walk** to scan the host.

The following screenshot shows the result of an SNMP Walk on a network device:

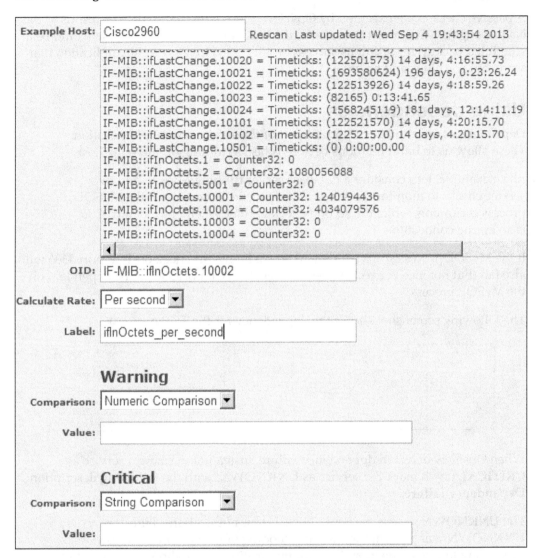

Once the SNMP Walk is completed, simply enter the OID you are interested in, add a label, and set some thresholds by using the numeric or string comparisons.

Passive

A passive check is not executed by Opsview, but is expected to deliver results to the Nagios engine using, most commonly, the **NSCA** interface. An example would be a scheduled backup reporting its success or failure to Opsview or an application that sends out warnings and so on.

Using dependencies

Dependencies are another important part of the service check configuration. These allow us to build relations between checks running on the same host.

As an example, let's consider a database server running MySQL and two service checks to monitor the server. The first check monitors if the MySQL process is running, while the second check verifies whether TCP port 3306 is accepting connections.

If the MySQL process stops running, then we know our check on TCP port 3306 will also fail (but not vice versa). So, we can consider TCP port 3306 to be dependent on the MySQL process.

The following screenshot shows the dependency for the TCP port 3306.

When Opsview detects a dependency failure, instead of marking a service as **CRITICAL** it will mark the service as **UNKNOWN**, with the following description: **Dependency failure**.

The **UNKNOWN** state is particularly useful for notifications. Filtering out **UNKNOWN** will prevent the instance flooding of the system administrator by sending him only the most relevant notifications. This allows us to quickly scan a host to find the main issue (root cause analysis). All other possible states are discussed in the *Configuring notifications* section in *Chapter 3, Advanced Configuration*.

It is highly recommended to use dependencies when you create your checks, as they will help you narrow down issues faster and more efficiently.

Adding plugins to the system

Even though Opsview comes with a huge amount of plugins already installed, you might want to add some new ones. This could be a plugin you created yourself, one you found on a website, or a plugin provided to you by suppliers or vendors. A great source of plugins is the Nagios Exchange (http://exchange.nagios.org).

The following steps explain how to add a new plugin and will make sure the plugin operates correctly in Opsview.

1. Download the plugin to your Opsview system using Wget or scp.

2. Make sure the plugin runs. You can check this by logging in to the Opsview system via SSH and running su - nagios to become the Nagios user before we can start testing the plugin.

   Another thing to check is whether the plugin has a help function. This is used by Opsview to fill the help page in the service check screen. It can be checked by running the plugin with the -h option.

 When testing plugins, always perform this as the Nagios user and from the Nagios user's home directory. This will prevent things from going wrong later on.

3. Once tested, simply copy the plugin (as the Nagios user, so the plugin will have the correct permissions) to the libexec directory under /usr/local/nagios of the Opsview system.

   Opsview keeps track of the libexec directory, but not the subdirectories. When it detects a change, it will rescan the directory for any new plugins and add them to the database, after which you can select the plugin from the drop-down menu.

   This usually takes less than a minute; running the populate_db.pl command as the Nagios user will also update the system.

Any plugin that was created in accordance with the Nagios developer's guidelines (https://www.nagios-plugins.org/doc/guidelines.html) will work in Opsview.

Handling performance data

Performance data can give you valuable, long-term views of how a service is performing. A simple example of this is the response times of a web server, too slow and customers will leave our website (and visit a competitor instead); so keeping track of this is paramount.

Any plugin that returns performance data (not all do) will be detected and performance graphs will be automatically made. As shown in the following screenshot, a graph icon will be added to the service check in the **monitoring** screen to show that performance data is available:

 Please note that the graph icon will become available after Opsview has received at least one result containing performance data and has been reloaded after receiving them. This will update the web interface.

Clicking on the icon will take you to a graph like the one shown in the following screenshot, which shows the memory utilization of the Opsview host.

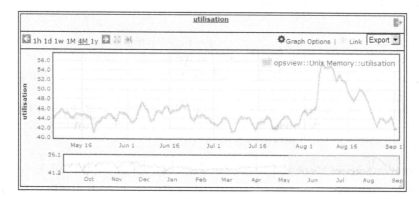

The image is dynamic, so you can select a time period from the timeline at the bottom, or you can zoom in to a specific time period in the graph.

In the graph, you can add additional sources that need to be incorporated into the graph. The graph will reset to its default when you leave the graph page. So, have a look at the various options and the export function.

Creating and installing Opspacks

Once you have created all kinds of host templates, service checks, and plugins, there might be times that you wish to copy them to another Opsview system or keep a backup.

Opspacks is a lesser known feature of Opsview. They are tarballs containing the following items (some of these will be discussed in the next chapter):

- Plugins
- Keywords
- Service groups
- Attributes
- Service checks
- Host templates

To create an Opspack, simply update your Opsview system with host templates, plugins, and so on. Then log in to your system using SSH and become the Nagios user (or log in as the Nagios user directly).

Running the following command will create a subdirectory in your current directory, which is named after the specified host template:

```
/usr/local/nagios/bin/create_opspack --username=admin --password=initial
'host template name'
```

On successful execution of the command, go to the new subdirectory and edit the info file if needed. The info file contains the version number, describes any dependencies, or tells you which version of Opsview is required.

Then, simply run the following command to create a tarball:

```
make mpack
```

You can now send the tarball to your other system and install it there using the following command:

```
/usr/local/nagios/bin/install_opspack tarball_name
```

As you can see, exporting and importing host templates (and their associated checks, attributes, and so on) is very easy and you can use this method to create Opspacks for any host template you have created.

Summary

We have covered quite some ground here looking at the basics of host templates, host groups, and hosts, and how to organize them.

We covered service checks in all their possible forms, dependencies, and performance data. We used a great tool, Opspacks, for exporting and importing templates.

In the next chapter we will look at more advanced features that come with Opsview and can be used within our monitoring system.

3
Advanced Configuration

So now that we have covered some of the basics of Opsview, let's have a look at some of the advanced features that Opsview offers us to improve our monitoring setup.

This will include the following:

- Using exceptions to override service checks
- Creating special **keyword** views for our users
- Using special host attributes to allow for specific situations and fast configuration
- Sending out **notifications** using notification profiles
- Using the test function in the web frontend
- Creating some advanced configurations for multi-homed systems and network outages
- Using the **REST API** for automation

Using exceptions

Now that we have discussed the service checks and host templates, it is time to look into a special feature of Opsview called **exceptions**.

Exceptions allow you to deviate from the regular settings of a service check, allowing you to customize without having to create a new service check.

You can set exceptions from the **Monitors** tab in the host template or on a host (exceptions on a host override those made through a host template).

In the following screenshot, we can see two exceptions: first, a timed exception and second, a regular exception:

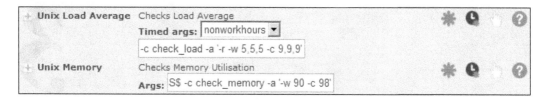

The timed exception will run during the interval that we we select with the arguments that are supplied and run normally outside of the interval. This allows us to set thresholds that are a bit higher, during nightly backups, for instance.

The regular exception simply overrules the regular service check (that might have been assigned using a host template) using the arguments supplied.

Use cases are higher loads during backups or a variation on a threshold or some other argument.

This allows us to configure a base service check that can be overridden based on a host template or based on the host if needed.

Creating and using keywords

A common issue in monitoring software is the grouping of information, and although Opsview already has good methods of grouping (host groups and service groups), it does present us with a limitation.

Let's consider a database server running multiple databases; one of them belongs to HRM and the other belongs to our financial system. Each database is used by special application servers (for example, one for HRM and one for Financial).

Since a host can only belong to one host group, we cannot place the database server in the HRM host group or the Financial host group without having the respective administrators for each group to have access to the whole host group.

Opsview solved this by introducing keywords. Keywords allow you to tag different service checks on different hosts (and in different host groups) with a specific word that you can then group into a **Keyword** view.

In this case, we would create two keywords by navigating to the **Keywords** menu via **settings | Advanced,** one for **HRM** and one for **Financial**. The creation for the **HRM** keyword is shown in the following screenshot:

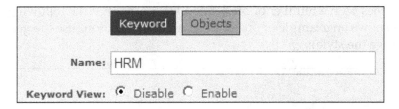

Using this keyword, we can then tag all the services on the database server that are related to HRM, and for Financial, we can use its respective keyword (the same applies for any service on their application servers).

We can perform this tagging from the **Edit keyword** page (under **Objects**) or on the **Edit host** or **Edit service check** pages.

 A service or host can have multiple keywords.

Using keyword views

When we enable the **Keyword View** setting from the **Edit keyword** screen, a number of options appear, as shown in the following screenshot:

Once enabled, you will be able to view all the hosts and services in various ways, depending on the style chosen, by navigating to **Monitoring | Status Summary | Keywords**.

Opsview comes with a number of predefined keywords, and the following screenshot shows an example of one of them as an illustration (use the gear icon to change the style):

Keywords are an extremely powerful way of grouping information that would be spread out over multiple host groups in other cases. They are used to get a single view of an application that might be spread out over hundreds of servers that are running across various parts of the application.

An additional and very important part of using keywords is the fact that we can use them as an access and notification filter; you can use it to make a role that only has access to a particular keyword or only receives notifications for a particular keyword.

Deploying keywords for grouping services and access control is easy, so I encourage you to try them out.

Creating and using host attributes

Host attributes allow you to create standardized service checks (one size fits all) and by using host attributes, you can tailor them to fit specific host needs.

This is an extremely powerful feature in Opsview as it allows you to make a single check that serves many hosts instead of many checks that each serve a small number of hosts.

Imagine the database server that was mentioned in *Chapter 2, Basic Configuration*, running an HRM and a Financial database. We might want to check if we can run a query on those specific databases, but for security reasons, we are not allowed to use the same username and password for both the databases. Normally this would mean creating two service checks, but by using host attributes, we can make do with a single service check.

Opsview comes with a number of predefined host attributes.

Here we can see the predefined attribute, **MYSQLCREDENTIALS**, which we can use simply by going to **settings | Basic | hosts**, selecting our host, and navigating to the **Attributes** tab. By clicking on the plus sign, we can add new attributes, as shown in the following screenshot:

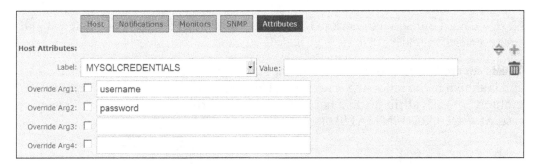

The **Value** field has some limitations on characters while the **Arg** fields have no limitations (if the **Arg** fields are hidden, click on the eye icon to make them visible).

 It is also possible to set a default value and arguments for an attribute, which will be applied to all checks using that attribute, by navigating to **settings | Advanced | Attributes**. If an attribute is assigned to a host (and the **Override** checkboxes are selected), the host's assigned values take precedence over the default values.

Of course, we need some way of accessing these values and arguments in our service checks, and Opsview does this by placing them into a macro.

To access the **Value** field (where we could, for instance, store the database name) shown in the screenshot, we would use the macro, `%MYSQLCREDENTIALS%`.

To access the first Argument (**Arg1**), we would use the macro, `%MYSQLCREDENTIALS:1%` (and substitute `1` with `2` for **Arg2**, and so on).

Our regular service check would look something like this:

```
check_mysql -H $HOSTADDRESS$ -u myhrmuser -p myhrmpassword -d HRM
```

Using attributes, the same check becomes:

```
check_mysql -H $HOSTADDRESS$ -u %MYSQCREDENTIALS:1% -p
%MYSQLCREDENTIALS:2% -d %MYSQLCREDENTIALS%
```

Using attributes to multiply service checks

You can assign the MYSQLCREDENTIALS attribute (or any other attribute) to a host as often as you want.

In our example, our database server runs two databases, so we need to assign the attribute twice—once for each database.

Next, we need our service check to spot the multiple attributes that we assigned and create a check for each attribute.

This is covered in the **Advanced** tab of the service check that will use the attribute and is shown in the following screenshot. Here we can set the check to automatically multiply for each attribute on a host (based on the attribute that we select; in this case, **MYSQL CREDENTIALS**).

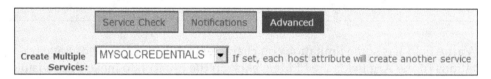

Using attributes is a great way of keeping the number of service checks down as we don't need a new check each time an argument in the check changes, and setting default values helps as we now only need to configure the hosts that need different values, thus saving us a lot of time configuring hosts.

You can use, create, and apply as many attributes as you want within Opsview and typical use cases include username and password, database names and credentials, port information, and so on.

Configuring notifications

Now, having all this monitoring power at your disposal is great; but what if you would like it to alert you when something is wrong, so that you don't have to watch the screen every second?

This is where the notifications come in, as Opsview allows each user to define their own notification profile or use a shared profile (which can be assigned by an admin).

The most common form of notification is to notify by e-mail.

For the **notify_by_email** functionality to work, the system must be able to send e-mails as the user Nagios.

To test if the e-mail is configured correctly, run the following command as the user `nagios`:

```
'date | /usr/bin/Mail -s "Subject" user@address'
```

To test the e-mail notifications from Opsview, run the following command (this will use the default template in Opsview to send additional information):

```
/usr/local/nagios/utils/test_notifications hostproblem
/usr/local/nagios/libexec/notifications/notify_by_email -t
```

The e-mail template is written in Template Toolkit (see `http://template-toolkit.org` for more information), and you can customize this or create your own template.

Opsview comes with notification scripts for e-mail, RSS, Googletalk, and SMS using AQL.

You can also add your own notification scripts by placing them in the `/usr/local/nagios/libexec/notifications` directory of your Opsview system and adding them through the **settings | Administration | Notification Methods**.

Using the `test_notifications` script, you can verify whether it is in working order or not.

You can create your own notification profile with your own personal settings. To do so, you click on the **Access Profile** option, as shown in the following screenshot:

After this, you click on the **Notifications** tab, fill in any needed fields (such as **Email**), and click on **Personal notification profiles**, as shown in the following screenshot:

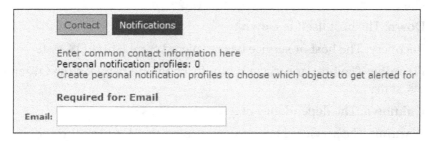

Then, you simply input a name and select the notification method (**Notify by:**), as shown in the following screenshot:

Name:	MyNotifications
Notify by:	☑ Email
	☐ RSS
	☐ Push Notifications For iOS Mobile

The next step is selecting the option for which you want to receive notifications.

The process is similar to selecting the status objects that are used to grant access to users, as we discussed in *Chapter 1, Opsview Core Basics*.

Selections can be made on host groups, service groups, and/or keywords.

As a final step, set the **Notify for** settings, shown in the following screenshot, to match your requirements (for instance, change the notification period or only notify on certain states such as **Critical**).

Let's run through the various states that will help in determining the notifications that you wish to receive:

- **Unreachable**: The parent of this host is **Down**
- **Down**: The host itself is **Down**
- **Recovery**: The host or service has recovered from a non-OK state
- **Flapping**: The host or service is rapidly changing between the **OK** and non-OK states
- **Unknown**: The dependency of a service is **Down**
- **Warning**: The service check results are over the **Warning** threshold
- **Critical**: The service check results are over the **Critical** threshold

Using shared notification profiles

Opsview offers the possibility to create shared profiles that you assign to roles (users can still create their own specific profiles).

Simply go to **settings | Administration | shared notification profiles** to create a profile; it works exactly like creating a personal notification profile.

A good example is having a shared notification profile for the on-call support assigned to the whole team during non-work hours, while employees can have their own notification profiles during the day.

Testing from the WebUI

Sometimes we find that after creating a service check we might need to tweak some settings (usually thresholds), but running all kinds of variations from the command-line might not be possible (for instance, if you want your users to test and come up with recommendations).

Opsview has three specific privileges that you can assign to a role for this case (in the **Status Access** tab of the role), and these are **TESTSOME, TESTALL,** and **TESTCHANGE**.

Of these three, the **TESTCHANGE** setting is the most important as it allows the users to modify parameters before executing the test (so they can, for instance, test various warnings or critical thresholds).

You can access the test feature from the contextual menu on any service check, as shown in the following screenshot:

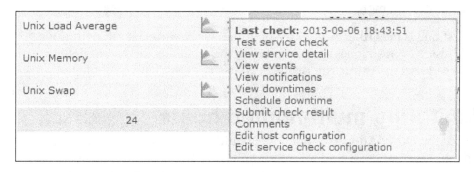

By clicking on **Test service check**, you will be able to run the check, as shown in the following screenshot. This role has **TESTCHANGE**; so, we can modify the arguments for this check, allowing us to test new settings without having to reload first; also, note the two **Help** functions.

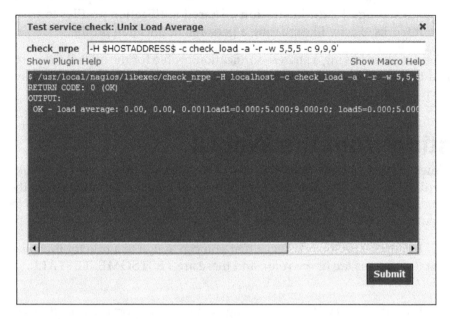

Using the advanced host configuration

Opsview offers an advanced way of defining hosts, and we have already seen some of these, such as exceptions, the SNMP setup, and host attributes; however, there is more.

The first one is the **Other Addresses** field that we can use to assign multiple IP addresses or hostnames to our host, and the second is the parent field that allows us to set up a structure that we can use to detect network outages.

Monitoring multi-homed hosts

Without the **Other Addresses** field, we would have to create unique hosts for each interface that we would like to monitor (in some cases, this can be a plus). This means that we need to maintain different configurations for each IP.

If your hosts are set up in an environment with a separate management and production network for instance, using **Other Addresses** allows you to keep all the checks within a single host, giving you a single view of that host.

To use this, go to **settings | Basic | hosts**, select your host to edit, and fill in any additional addresses that your host may have, as shown in the following screenshot (for clarity, we have used IPs but using hostnames is perfectly fine):

| Other Hostnames/IPs: | 10.0.0.1,127.0.0.1,172.16.0.1,192.168.1.1 |
| | Other network addresses for this host, comma separated |

To use these addresses in our service check, Opsview (such as host attributes) uses a macro to make them available; to use the first address, simply use the macro $ADDRESS1$, for the second use $ADDRESS2$, and so on.

Remember the service check that we discussed while looking at **host attributes**. Well, here's the same service check, but now we want it to run against the third IP address. So, we input the correct macro and we are done.

```
check_mysql -H $ADDRESS3$ -u %MYSQCREDENTIALS:1% -p
%MYSQLCREDENTIALS:2% -d %MYSQLCREDENTIALS%
```

Using parenting for network outage detection

Much like the dependencies that we discussed in the *Using dependencies* section of *Chapter 2, Basic Configuration,* to make logical relations between services, the same can be applied to the network used to reach our hosts.

Let's assume that our Opsview server is connected to switchA. RouterA is also connected to switchA. So, if switchA fails from the Opsview server's point of view, RouterA becomes unreachable.

> **Unreachable** simply means that there is another issue that prevents us from determining the real state of our host.
>
> You can turn the notifications on and off for the **Unreachable** field in your **Notification** profile. Turning it off will prevent a lot of notifications during network outages.

To set up this relationship, we first need to edit the host, **switchA** from **settings | Basic | Hosts**, and we have defined Opsview as its parent, as shown in the following screenshot:

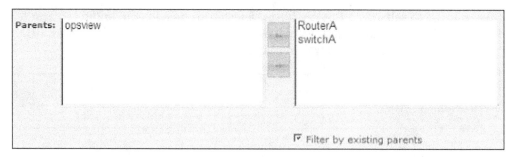

Once submitted, we then edit the host, **RouterA,** and add **switchA** as its parent, as shown in the following screenshot:

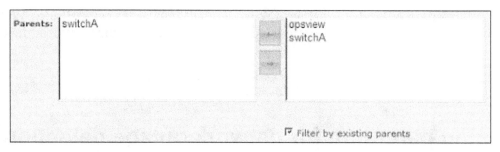

After applying the changes through the **settings** menu, we can see our newly set up relations from the **Monitoring | Status Detail | Network** screen, as shown in the following screenshot:

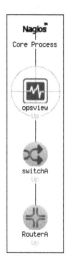

Using parenting can really help while trying to figure out why a certain host (or hosts) have gone **DOWN** by letting Opsview detect if there is an issue with the network. It can also save you loads of notifications (which can be overwhelming if, for instance, a data center switch connecting hundreds of hosts fails).

The fastest and easiest way of determining the path from Opsview to any host is to simply run `traceroute` from the Opsview server and duplicate the path in Opsview.

Automation with the REST API

Being able to automate various actions can save you a lot of time that you would otherwise spend on adding hosts, contacts, or service checks, for instance.

Try running the following command that will output the configuration for the Opsview server:

```
/usr/local/nagios/bin/opsview_rest --username=admin --password=initial
--pretty --data-format=json GET config/host?s.name=opsview
```

The REST API is able to perform nearly any task that you can do using the web interface, so it is a great tool for those looking into automation.

Configuration

You can add contacts, hosts, host templates and host groups, service groups, notification methods, attributes and keywords, time periods, and so on using the REST API.

The following are some examples that you can run to see various objects; if you redirect the output into a file, you can edit and import it using the PUT request instead of the GET request.

The following is an example of using the json filter to find all the contacts that have admin in their name:

```
/usr/local/nagios/bin/opsview_rest --username=admin --password=initial
--pretty --data-format=json GET
'config/contact?json_filter={"name":{"-like":"%25admin%25"}}'
```

An example to retrieve all attributes is as follows:

```
/usr/local/nagios/bin/opsview_rest --username=admin --password=initial
--pretty --data-format=json GET config/attribute
```

These are just small samples of what is possible using the REST API for configuration. See the REST API conclusion section on where to find more information about the API.

Informational objects

The following four objects that we will look into are only used to retrieve information, so only the GET operations are supported.

- **Status**: We can retrieve the current state of any host or service on the Opsview system using the status object.

  The following is an example for retrieving the current status of our Opsview server:

  ```
  /usr/local/nagios/bin/opsview_rest --username=admin
  --password=initial --pretty --data-format=json GET
  status/host?host=opsview
  ```

- **Runtime**: This object allows us to query Opsview for any hosts or services that are currently being used by Opsview, and an example to retrieve the list of services that Opsview is currently using to monitor our environment is shown here:

  ```
  /usr/local/nagios/bin/opsview_rest --username=admin
  --password=initial --pretty --data-format=json GET
  runtime/service
  ```

- **Graphs**: As we have seen, Opsview creates performance graphs for any service that returns performance data. We can retrieve this information from Opsview using the graph REST API object.

  Here's an example to retrieve one week's worth of data for the response time on the Opsview HTTP check.

  ```
  /usr/local/nagios/bin/opsview_rest --username=admin
  --password=initial --pretty --data-format=json GET
  'graph?hsm=opsview::Opsview HTTP::time&duration=1w'
  ```

- **Events**: Closely tied into this object is the view that we get by navigating to **Monitoring | Status Summary | Events**, which is a visual representation of this data.

  Here's an example to retrieve the events for the Unix Swap service check on the Opsview host.

  ```
  /usr/local/nagios/bin/opsview_rest --username=admin
  --password=initial --pretty --data-format=json GET
  'event?service=Unix Swap&host=opsview'
  ```

- **Actionable objects**: The next three objects allow us to take specific actions, so they not only use GET but also the POST or PUT functions.

  - ° **Rechecks**: A recheck will force Opsview to immediately re-run the check to get the latest information and can be applied on a single service or all services for a specific host.

    Here is an example that will force Opsview to re-run all checks on a given host:

    ```
    /usr/local/nagios/bin/opsview_rest --username=admin
    --password=initial --pretty POST "recheck?hostname=opsview&s
    ervicename=%"
    ```

  - ° **Downtime**: This object allows us to mark a host, host group, or service as being "down for maintenance" that will suppress notifications during the time period defined (but not the execution of checks against that host, host group, or service).

    We can list (GET), add (PUT), and remove (DELETE) downtime that is set using the contextual menu and vice versa using the REST API.

    Try setting some downtime on the Opsview host using the contextual menu in the web interface and then run the following example to retrieve it using the REST API.

    ```
    /usr/local/nagios/bin/opsview_rest --username=admin
    --password=initial --pretty --data-format=json GET
    'downtime?host=opsview'
    ```

  - ° **Acknowledge**: Similar to downtime, acknowledgements can be set to suppress notifications but are more commonly used to indicate that we are aware of a particular issue (service check failing) and are working on a resolution.

    We can retrieve (GET) a list of acknowledgements or add (PUT) them to our Opsview system using the REST API.

    The following example will list all the checks that we can acknowledge on the host Opsview:

    ```
    /usr/local/nagios/bin/opsview_rest --username=admin
    --password=initial --pretty --data-format=json GET
    'acknowledge?host=opsview'
    ```

Wrapping up the REST API

This has just been a small sample containing some of the most important parts of the REST API; so if you are looking into automation in combination with Opsview, the REST API is a good starting point (see `http://docs.opsview.com/doku.php?id=opsview-core:restapi` for more information on the REST API).

If you are running the Puppet configuration management tool, there is an available module for Opsview that you can use to automatically add new hosts and uses the REST API as its interface with Opsview (see `http://forge.puppetlabs.com/opsview/opsview` for more information).

Summary

This has been a very packed chapter that covered a lot of exciting features that Opsview offers its users to help them get the most out of monitoring.

We have addressed some of the challenges that we face today in increasingly complex multi-homed environments and how we can resolve them using Opsview.

In the next chapter, we will be looking at agents, agentless deployments, and new technologies such as virtualization and cloud, as well as some of the modules that are currently used in Opsview Core.

Agents, Clouds, and Modules

So far we have mainly focused on the server side of Opsview and have looked at what it can do for us to make monitoring more effective and easy to maintain.

In this chapter, we will be looking at servers and services that we would like to monitor and some of the considerations on how we can monitor them.

We will also look at some of the modules you can use that are currently part of Opsview Core.

Using agents

Opsview offers agents for various platforms such as Linux and Windows, so check out the **Downloads** page on the Opsview website to get the most current version for your platform (see *Chapter 1, Opsview Core Basics*, for the URL of the download page).

If you are moving from a Nagios-based deployment to Opsview, you can simply recycle the agents as Opsview supports any **NRPE** (**Nagios Remote Plugin Executor**) or NSClient++ agent.

The decision to deploy agents largely depends on how you wish to execute your checks. Some checks might need to run locally on the host (for this, we need an agent), while others might only need remote access (through **SNMP** or **SSH** for instance) in which case we could monitor without the need for an agent.

Other considerations could be that of security, multi-homed environments, available resources, and even legal considerations (maybe a support party will not provide support if you install additional software on their system).

In most cases, deploying agents is the most suitable solution; it allows you to have the most flexible setup as, by doing so, the agent can be easily modified to perform new checks and use new plugins.

Adding plugins to the Linux agent

To add a new plugin to the Opsview agent on a Linux-based system, simply drop the executable plugin in /usr/local/nagios/libexec on the target host. Then add a file to the nrpe_local directory in /usr/local/nagios/etc/ with the following syntax:

```
command[check_my_plugin]=/usr/local/nagios/libexec/check_my_plugin
$ARG1$
```

Save the file, restart the Opsview agent (using the command service opsview-agent restart for instance), and you can now use your new check.

 Using just $ARG1$ in your agent configuration has a great advantage in that you only need to change arguments within Opsview and not on every agent when changes are required.

Adding plugins to the Windows agent

For the Windows Opsview agent, we follow a similar but slightly more complex process.

Depending on what language your script was written in (as a batch script, a Powershell script, or maybe even a Perl script), make sure you use the correct extension: .vbs for Visual Basic, .ps1 for Powershell, .bat for batch files, and .pl for Perl files.

Drop the new plugin into the scripts directory of the Opsview Agent, and add the following line to the NSC.ini file in the **Wrapped Scripts** section.

```
myCheck=myScript.pl $ARG1$
```

Save the file and restart the agent from the **Windows Management Console**; you can now use your check.

Agentless monitoring

In some situations, we simply cannot deploy agents to perform all kinds of monitoring functions; the most common cases are those of networking equipment or appliances. But even when we cannot deploy an agent, we still wantto keep track of these hosts and to handle this, Opsview allows for various forms of agentless monitoring.

SSH

The `SSH` method of performing remote monitoring is based on using `check_by_ssh` as a plugin, connecting to our host using SSH, and then performing an action.

This action can be used to run a single command or execute a script and return the results of these actions to Opsview.

Setting up SSH checks follows the same principles as any service check in Opsview, and a number of examples are included in the installation guide.

To use `check_by_ssh`, you will need to set up a remote user (the same user that the plugin will use when logging in) and make sure SSH keys are exchanged so the login is performed without passwords. As this might constitute a security risk, make sure you really have no alternative to monitor in any other way.

On your remote host, create a user (the easiest way is to create the user Nagios).

On your Opsview system, generate SSH keys for the Nagios user (without a pass phrase) by running the following commands:

```
su - nagios
ssh-keygen -t dsa
```

Then, copy the public key to your remote system using the following command:

```
ssh-copy-id -i ~/.ssh/id_dsa.pub <FQDN or IP of remote system>
```

SNMP and host interfaces

Using SNMP is most commonly applied to network equipment, and Opsview comes with a number of host templates to perform this: **OS - Linux SNMP** and **SNMP - MIB II**. It is also part of the **host interfaces** feature of Opsview.

To use this, simply add the host from **settings | Basic | hosts**, configure the **Primary Hostname/IP** and the **Host Title** fields, assign any of the host templates you want, and go to the **SNMP** tab to configure the right community (or username and password when using SNMP v3). Always verify whether your configuration is correct using **Test SNMP connection** (if the test fails, check the remote host for any configuration mishaps).

Depending on the type of device, consult your vendor documentation on configuring SNMP that usually includes items such as community and **Access Control Lists** (**ACLs**).

Opsview makes adding network devices very easy using the **SNMP - MIB II** host template in combination with host interfaces.

From the SNMP tab, click on **Submit and edit host interfaces**, which will bring up the host interfaces screen. Simply click on **Query Host** to scan the host for any interfaces, make a selection of the interfaces you wish to monitor (or all), set thresholds, and submit the query; the following screenshot shows a section of the host interfaces screen, allowing us to select the interfaces and set various thresholds for alerts:

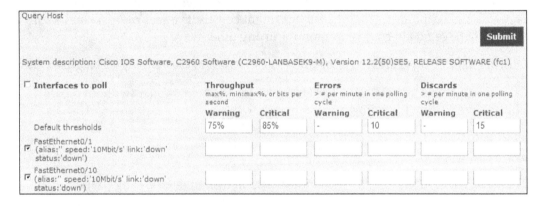

Once set up (and after some polling has been done), navigate to **monitoring | Status Summary | Host Groups** and drill down to your host.

From the contextual menu, select **View host interfaces**, which will display all monitored interfaces, including graphs, in an attractive manner.

Creating your own SNMP-based templates is easy using the method that we discussed in the *SNMP polling* section in *Chapter 2, Basic Configuration*, or by using some of the SNMP-based plugins that come with Opsview.

WMI

Windows Management Instrumentation (WMI) is another method of running agentless checks. You can find more information about WMI at `http://technet. microsoft.com`. Opsview has included the basic binaries and libraries needed to run WMI checks from an Opsview system, so all that we need to do is add the correct plugin to make use of WMI.

You can install the plugin by downloading it from `http://exchange.nagios. org/directory/Plugins/Operating-Systems/Windows/WMI/Check-WMI-Plus/ details` and placing it in the `libexec` directory at `/usr/local/nagios/` as described in the *Adding plugins to the system*, in *Chapter 2, Basic Configuration*.

> The `check_wmi_plus` plugin comes with a number of predefined checks, so you can use these to create your service checks and host templates.

Next you will need to create a user on your Windows hosts that allows for WMI access, or create a domain-based account if all your hosts are on a Windows domain.

See `http://www.edcint.co.nz/checkwmiplus/?q=configurewindowsfromops` for more information on configuring access for **check_wmi_plus**.

Once completed, you should now be able to run checks against Windows hosts using WMI.

The following is an example you could try to run from the Opsview host; substitute $HOSTADDRESS$ with the Windows host you want to check and input the correct username and password:

```
/usr/local/nagios/libexec/check_wmi_plus.pl -H $HOSTADDRESS$ -m
sample -s minimal -u username -p password
```

If everything is working, you should receive the result **OK** and the Windows version that is running on the remote host.

> The Opsview Pro and Enterprise versions come with predefined host templates, service checks, and plugins for WMI monitoring.

Virtualization and Cloud monitoring

Out of the box, Opsview offers host templates and service checks aimed at monitoring virtual systems and Cloud-based systems.

Virtualization

As virtualization has taken flight, we need some way of monitoring the main environment of our virtual platform (any guests could be monitored using the Opsview agent to get extra information). For this, Opsview offers a series of service checks that you can use to monitor Xen, KVM, and VMware (using SNMP for VMware), which you can also use to create host templates depending on the platform you use.

Setting up vSphere monitoring

A more comprehensive way of monitoring VMware ESX can be easily integrated into Opsview using VMware's **vSphere Perl SDK** in combination with the `check_vmware_api` plugin, which uses the API in VMware's products to retrieve information.

First, install the vSphere Perl SDK by downloading it from the VMware site (make sure you follow the installation instructions carefully); go to the following URL for the latest version of the vSphere Perl SDK: `https://communities.vmware.com/community/vmtn/developer/forums/vsphere_sdk_perl`.

Then download the `check_vmware_api` plugin from `http://exchange.nagios.org/directory/Plugins/Operating-Systems/%2A-Virtual-Environments/VMWare/check_vmware_api/details`.

Add the plugin to your Opsview system like you would add any other plugin, and create the service checks and host templates you require.

> The Opsview Pro and Enterprise versions come with predefined host templates and service checks for VMware, but you will have to install the vSphere Perl SDK, which cannot be shipped with Opsview for legal reasons.

Being able to monitor your ESX servers can help you keep track of your resources and bottlenecks, while monitoring each VM individually (using the Opsview agent for instance) will help you track down the VMs responsible for the most resource claims.

Cloud monitoring

When running applications or services from the cloud, it is important to keep track of them and not solely rely on your SLA with your provider. To do so, Opsview offers host templates for two common cloud providers, Slicehost and Amazon AWS, which you can use to keep track of the health of your cloud services.

Amazon AWS

To monitor your Amazon Web Services, Opsview comes with three predefined service checks.

The first check shown here will simply monitor the number of running instances on your Amazon EC2 and go critical if less than one or more than two instances are running.

```
check_aws_ec2_instances -k %AWS_ACCESS_KEY% -s %AWS_SECRET_KEY% -c
1:2
```

As you can see, the check uses attributes for the access key and the secret key, so make sure you assign these attributes to your host (or set the defaults via **settings | Advanced | Attributes**).

 If you are using AWS with auto-scaling, consider using a timed exception with higher thresholds, during peak hours for instance.

The second check that we will see in a bit will make sure your instances are running correctly. This check uses similar attributes and introduces a new attribute to designate the instance we are interested in, as we can see here:

```
check_aws_ec2 -k %AWS_ACCESS_KEY% -s %AWS_SECRET_KEY% -i
%AWS_INSTANCE% -w pending,shutting_down,stopping -o running
```

By default, this check is set to multiply (we discussed the **Multiple** setting in the *Using attributes to multiply service checks* section in *Chapter 3, Advanced Configuration*) each AWS_INSTANCE attribute assigned to your host.

The last check shown here is designed to keep track of the state of your S3 buckets (or web-based storage), and it uses the AWS_BUCKET_NAME attribute to allow for multiple checks on a single host.

```
check_aws_s3 -k %AWS_ACCESS_KEY% -s %AWS_SECRET_KEY% -n
%AWS_BUCKET_NAME%
```

Slicehost

Opsview also comes with two service checks for monitoring a Slicehost. Both of these services use the SLICEHOST_NAME attribute to multiply checks when we need to check for more than one host.

The following check will report on bandwidth usage for the given Slicehost:

```
check_slicehost -k %SLICEHOST_KEY:1% -n %SLICEHOST_NAME% --bandwidth
```

The status check will check whether the given Slicehost is in an active state.

```
check_slicehost -k %SLICEHOST_KEY:1% -n %SLICEHOST_NAME% --status
```

Note that the SLICEHOST_KEY attribute will use the first argument instead of the value.

Clouds on the horizon

As more and more cloud operators start up, being able to effectively monitor your services becomes paramount. So even though we have just looked at two providers, new plugins are being developed to monitor any new providers that you can add and operate from your Opsview installation.

Using core modules

Opsview Core comes with a number of preinstalled third-party modules that you can use for visualization or to keep track of network devices.

The following image shows the list of modules that are enabled in Opsview Core taken from the **Modules** list via **settings | Administration**.

	Module	Installed	Description
🗑 📑	Nagvis	Yes	Nagios Core Visualisation /modules/nagvis
🗑 📑	MRTG	Yes	Multi Router Traffic Grapher /status/network_traffic
🗑 📑	NMIS	Yes	Network Management Information System /cgi-nmis/nmiscgi.pl

Activating a module (or deactivating a module) can be achieved by selecting it from the menu and updating the settings as shown in the following screenshot for the **NMIS** module:

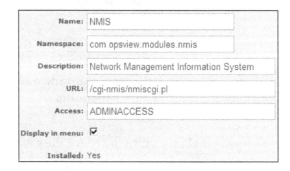

Both NMIS and MRTG have been superseded in part by the **host interfaces** functionality in Opsview, which we have briefly discussed in the *SNMP and host interfaces* section of this chapter.

NagVis

NagVis is a simple visualization tool that offers some basic icons and uses a reasonably simple menu to create maps on which you can create views of your environment. For more information on NagVis, go to `http://www.nagvis.org`.

The following screenshot is from the **Automap** feature, which comes with NagVis showing a map similar to the map generated in the **Network** view via **monitoring | Status Detail**.

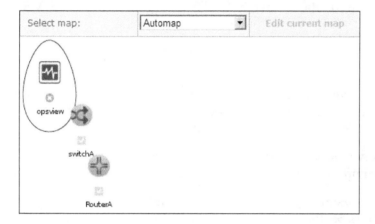

Through NagVis, you can create more detailed views using any service check as input for icons.

MRTG

The **Multi Router Traffic Grapher** (**MRTG**) is specialized in making graphs for network devices and for allowing you to search through these graphs using a simple search function, and then use RRD graphs for further examinations. MRTG does not have any alerting capabilities, which are available when using the Opsview **host interfaces** feature we discussed in the *SNMP and host interfaces* section of this chapter. For more information on MRTG, go to `http://oss.oetiker.ch/mrtg/`.

To have MRTG generate graphs (it uses its own poll cycle to retrieve interface statistics), simply enable it in the SNMP section of the host configuration. Note that having MRTG enabled for a lot of hosts will have an impact on the overall system performance. In the following screenshot, we can see MRTG has been enabled for our host:

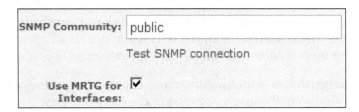

To access the information stored in MRTG, navigate to **modules | MRTG** and select the graphs you wish to view from the list of hosts being monitored by MRTG.

NMIS

The **Network Management Information System** (**NMIS**) is in many aspects similar to MRTG, but it will retrieve and generate a whole lot more information, including availability statistics and health measurements.

It does, however, lack an alert system, and while monitoring, many hosts with NMIS will have an impact on the overall system performance similar to that of MRTG.

To enable NMIS, simply check the box in the SNMP section of the host and select what type of host it is. So, for a switch, refer to the following screenshot:

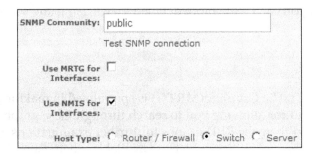

NMIS has a whole lot of different tools and measurements that you can view by navigating to **modules | NMIS**, which will take you to the NMIS main page.

Summary

The earlier chapters were all focused on the Opsview server, and we now had some time to look at the client side of monitoring. We saw some different ways of monitoring using agents or by monitoring agentless and using techniques such as WMI, SSH, and SNMP (including host interfaces). We had a quick look at virtualization and Cloud-based checks that come with Opsview.

Finally we looked at the modules that are shipped with Opsview, which we can use to gather more information from our network or visualize our various systems.

In the next chapter, we will be looking at how we can use Opsview in combination with our smartphones or tablets to provide us with a permanent link to our system even when we are out of office.

5
Opsview Mobile

Another great feature of Opsview is that it comes with a mobile application for both iOS and Android devices. Being able to remotely check your IT estate, without having to go into the office or using a VPN from home, is a great feature.

Imagine a service check has just gone over its warning threshold; you log in using your mobile phone and determine it can wait until the next business day, after which you acknowledge the issue. This saves you a trip into the office.

In this chapter, we will look at both of these applications and how to configure them to give you access to your Opsview installation anytime and anywhere.

Configuring Opsview for Opsview Mobile

To use Opsview Mobile, the application on your phone or device needs access to the Opsview REST API. In most cases, this means opening up the Opsview web interface to the Internet (for instance, at a special website `www.opsview.mycompany.com`); and that's why using HTTPS is recommended. Opsview Mobile can handle self-signed certificates if you wish to use one.

Mobile phones connected to your LAN (using wireless) should also be able to resolve the URL to be able to connect. So make sure you configure your environment, so that it can be used within the office and from outside (or if your security policy does not allow it, only when connected to the local WiFi network).

Opsview Mobile on Android

The mobile application is delivered as a native app for Android (Version 2.1 or later); so simply go to the app store, search for Opsview Mobile (or go to the following URL: `https://play.google.com/store/apps/details?id=com.opsview.android`), and select install.

Once the app is installed, we need to configure the app for our system. The following screenshot shows the settings screen, which has various items that we need to configure:

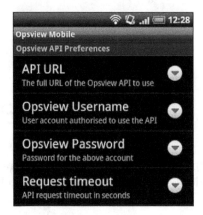

The **API URL** option is the site that you wish your mobile to connect to, and which we can enter by tapping on it. As per our earlier example, this would be `https://www.opsview.mycompany.com`, as shown in the following screenshot:

Then simply put in your **Opsview Username** and **Opsview Password** details (adjust the **Request timeout** settings if you are using really slow mobile services) and you are ready to go.

The default screen (once connected) is the host group hierarchy as shown in the following screenshot. You can navigate into the host group hierarchy by clicking on a group and then on a host to drill down into the services. Then, you can use the back button to return to the previous screen.

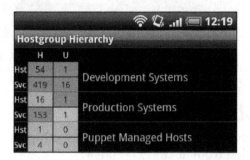

Pressing the menu button down for a couple of seconds will bring up the **Actions** menu. For example, if you are viewing a service, you could schedule a recheck, a refresh, or acknowledge the issue as shown in the following screenshot:

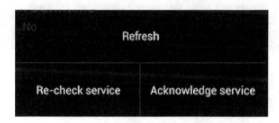

From the main screen, you can also go to the **Keyword** view by using the menu accessible by pressing down the menu button for a couple of seconds, as shown in the following screenshot:

As discussed in the *Creating and using keywords* section in *Chapter 3, Advanced Configuration,* we can use the **Keyword** view to create a single view of an entire application; for instance, your corporate website including load balancers, web servers, and the database backend.

The following screenshot shows an example of the two default keywords for the Opsview system:

Opsview Mobile on iOS

The iOS version of Opsview Mobile requires iOS 5.0 or higher to run. You can download the application from https://itunes.apple.com/us/app/opsview-mobile/id562228796. The menu structure, functions, and navigation is roughly the same for both applications. In the following screenshot, we can see the main menu that is used to navigate in iOS:

Opsview Mobile for iOS supports advanced graphs for displaying performance data. As shown in the following screenshot, you can view graphs using five different time periods:

Another feature of Opsview Mobile for iOS is its ability to receive **push notifications** from your Opsview system as an alternative to SMS or e-mail notifications.

Push notifications for Opsview Mobile is a free service offered by Opsview and uses HTTPS to securely transfer notification messages from your Opsview system to the Opsview push servers and on to your mobile device.

All notifications sent to Opsview contain the sending system's unique identifier. So, a mobile device needs to be connected to your Opsview system first before push notifications are configured (to retrieve the **UUID**).

The UUID and Opsview account information in the mobile phone application is then used by the push server to forward the correct notification to the correct device.

Using push notifications

There are a number of steps you need to take for using push notifications. They are given as follows:

1. First, we need a valid Opsview.com account. So, if you don't have one yet you can create one for free on their website. We need this to authenticate and send notifications to the Opsview push server.

2. You need to agree to the terms and conditions in order to create your account.

 Each user that wants to receive push notifications needs a valid Opsview.com account. However, you can use a single account to send out the push notifications.

3. Next, on your Opsview system, go to **settings | Administration | Notification Methods** and select **Push Notifications For IOS Mobile** to configure the push settings.

4. Enter the account registered on Opsview.com that you will be using to send the notifications to the Opsview push server. This does not have to be the same account that is configured in the application, but it must be a valid Opsview.com account.

5. As shown in the following screenshot, we have added the user that will send the notifications. If needed, we can add a proxy server to relay the traffic.

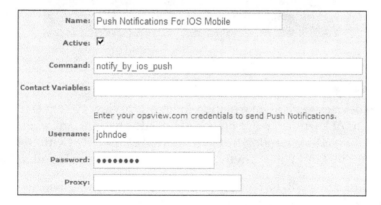

6. Your Opsview server needs to be able to connect to https://push.opsview.com, either directly or through a proxy server.

7. Open the Opsview Mobile application on your mobile phone and configure the **Opsview System Authentication** to match your account on your Opsview system.

8. In the **Push Notification Settings** on your mobile phone, configure the `Opsview.com` account that you have made for this phone. This account can be the same as the one we used in the notification method, but it could also be a different user account.

9. Once the mobile phone is configured, you can go to your **Access profile** on your Opsview system and add the **Push Notifications For iOS Mobile** method by selecting the **Notifications** tab followed by clicking on **Personal notification profiles**, as shown in the following screenshot:

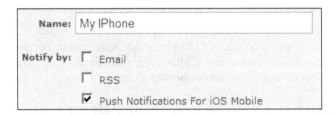

Once all steps have been completed, you will be able to receive notifications. An example of notifications received on an iPhone is shown here:

Summary

Using mobile devices to view information in your Opsview system can have great benefits in terms of keeping an eye on your IT estate anytime, anywhere. Various deployments are possible ranging from an internal office only (with Bring Your Own Device, for instance) or as anytime, anywhere; the choice is yours.

In the next chapter, we will be looking at troubleshooting our Opsview installation and how to use the various tools provided by Opsview to help us out.

6
The Three Ts

The Three Ts are **Testing**, **Tools**, and **Troubleshooting**. In this chapter, we will discuss tools and important parts of the Opsview system that will help us if we run into problems. Every once in a while, things will not work as intended (or expected) and so we need to have some tools available to help us figure out the cause.

In the *Testing from the WebUI* section in *Chapter 3*, *Advanced Configuration*, we have already seen how to test plugins from the web interface. But, sometimes we would like to test or debug directly on the server or client. In this chapter, we will look into how we can use the various tools that Opsview provides to help us troubleshoot, maintain, and debug our system.

 When operating on the command line of your Opsview server, always work as the user Nagios.

Running plugins or scripts as the user Nagios (using: `su -nagios`) will make sure you are running them with exactly the same settings as Opsview. It will also ensure any (temporary) files created by plugins or scripts have the correct privileges.

Let's start by looking at some tools that Opsview provides; some are for troubleshooting and some are tools that have more general functions.

Using the tools from the utils directory

The `/usr/local/nagios/utils` directory of Opsview comes with all kinds of scripts that we can use, and we will be looking at the most important ones here. But, feel free to look around and have a look at the others.

clone_host

The first tool that we will look at is the `clone_host` script, which allows us to quickly clone a host for an x number of times (the web interface clone option only allows us to make a single copy).

Here's an example, in which we will clone a host called `myhost` ten times. Once completed, go to **settings | Basic | Hosts** to view the new hosts.

```
/usr/local/nagios/utils/clone_host --username=admin
--password=initial --from=myhost --total=10
```

You can use the same script to delete hosts by setting the total to the number of hosts you wish to remain after the operation. Shown here is an example that will remove all hosts except one (use this with great care!):

```
/usr/local/nagios/utils/clone_host --username=admin
--password=initial --total=1 --delete
```

copy_host_attributes

Assuming that we already have hostA and hostB and we would like to copy any host attributes from hostA, we can use the `copy_host_attributes` script to do so. In the web interface, this would mean editing hostB and manually adding the attributes.

Here is an example to copy the attributes from `hostA` to `hostB`:

```
/usr/local/nagios/utils/copy_host_attributes hostA hostB
```

export_full_config

The `export_full_config` tool will create an output in JSON format for all objects in Opsview, except the hosts and plugins (hostgroups, attributes, timeperiods, keywords, and so on are included).

For instance, using this output you can import the configuration using the `import_json` tool into a new Opsview installation (in essence copying everything except the hosts). This allows you to quickly create new Opsview systems that are all ready to go.

export_host_template

The `export_host_template` tool will create a JSON-formatted overview of any host template, including service checks and service groups (similar to the Opspacks discussed in the *Creating and installing Opspacks* section in *Chapter 2, Basic Configuration*) but without any plugins.

Use the `import_json` tool to import it into a new Opsview installation. You can use this when you only need to copy a number of host templates and not the entire system (like with the previous command).

get_actual_command

The `get_actual_command` tool will generate a list of all checks assigned to a specific host, including all the arguments, similar to **Resolve service checks** in the contextual menu in the **Hosts** screen via **settings** | **Basic**.

Use this command to see the checks as they have last been executed by Opsview; simply run `get_actual_command <hostname>` to see a full list of checks.

list_unknown_devices

The `list_unknown_devices` tool will scan the logs for any host that is sending passive results, but which is not currently defined in Opsview.

Simply call `list_unknown_devices` and a list containing the unknown hosts will be returned.

rename_host

As all data for a host is stored based on its **Host Title** (graphs, for instance), renaming a host means losing these graphs. But, by using the `rename_host` function, any graphs associated with the host will also be moved along. This saves our valuable data.

test_notifications

The last tool we will mention here is the `test_notifications` script, which we can use to verify whether our newly added notification script works the way we want it to.

The example here shows how we send a `hostproblem` message to `my_notify_script`:

```
/usr/local/nagios/utils/test_notifications hostproblem
/usr/local/nagios/libexec/notifications/my_notify_script
```

We will then see some output detailing the information sent, and if everything goes well, we will receive our notification with the same information.

nlcat

We already discussed the `import_json` tool. Unlike the previous tools, it is not in the `utils` directory, but in the `/usr/local/nagios/bin` directory.

There is another great tool in the `bin` directory: `nlcat`. This tool will parse the `nagios.log` files and return the results depending on the used parameters.

Here's an example that shows us how to parse the last three log files for any occurrences of disk (note that `(?i)` makes the search case insensitive).

```
/usr/local/nagios/bin/nlcat -n 4 -l '(?i)disk'
```

The following example will search through the last three log files of the past ten days (ignoring the newer files).

```
/usr/local/nagios/bin/nlcat -n 10 -e 7 -l '(?i)disk'
```

The `-n` option will limit the log files searched to the last *n* number of logs. The `-l` option will print the line number of the file on which the query matched. The `-e` option will ignore the more recent log files. The `-p` is another great option that we can use. It will filter out some of the additional messages, only showing the entries that might be a problem.

Using this tool, we can easily search through the logs to see if certain events have taken place (such as, did we send out a notification to a specific user on a specific date?).

Testing plugins from the command line

Whenever we add a new plugin, figuring out the various options and arguments can be a lot of work, and doing this from the web interface might take too long.

Testing plugins from the command line speeds things up considerably. Once the plugin is installed (as discussed in the *Adding plugins to the system* section in *Chapter 2, Basic Configuration*), we can simply call it using various arguments.

So, logged in as the user Nagios, we start with a simple help call that should show all the arguments available in our plugin. This command assumes that the plugin was installed on our Opsview server.

```
/usr/local/nagios/libexec/check_my_plugin -h
```

If the plugin was installed on a remote host and the agent was updated to execute the plugin (as discussed in the *Using Agents* section in *Chapter 4, Agents, Clouds, and Modules*), then we would run the following command from our Opsview server:

```
/usr/local/nagios/libexec/check_nrpe -H <remote host> -c check_my_plugin
-a '-h'
```

This should show the `help` function of our plugin.

> Although a specific plugin might only be used on certain hosts, I do advise to also install them on the Opsview server as this will allow the web interface to maintain a list of all available plugins (including their usage information).
>
> This does not apply to Windows plugins (as they will not run on Linux) and of course plugins that contain sensitive information such as usernames or passwords.

Checking the various log files and debugging

There are a number of important log files within Opsview, which we can use when looking into issues. We can also modify the log levels on the fly in case we need more information.

Opsview log files

The log files for Opsview are located in the `/var/log/opsview` directory and are split into two files: the `opsviewd.log` file for any log messages related to the operations of Opsview, and the `opsview-web.log` file for any messages related to the web interface.

Opsviewd.log

When Opsview starts, it will run a number of important processes. Each process is responsible for various parts of the system, and each of these will report issues (if any) to the `opsviewd.log`file. We will quickly look at the most important processes here.

import_ndologsd

The `import_ndologsd` process is responsible for taking the results of checks from Nagios and inserting them into the Opsview runtime database. If this process fails to start, it will be reported in the `opsviewd.log`.

Without `import_ndologsd` running, the web interface will not be updated (each check in the web interface has a timestamp to verify this). So, if the web interface appears to be "behind", as in it shows old or outdated information, this is the first place you should look.

import_perfdatarrd

The `import_perfdatarrd` process is responsible for processing any performance data into RRD files; issues from this process will be reported in `opsviewd.log`. If the graphs have stopped updating, then check if there is an issue with `import_perfdatarrd`.

Opsview-web.log

Any events related to the web interface or the REST API are logged into the `opsview-web.log` file, which includes logins for users.

Debugging

By default, most processes will only report errors. But, sometimes we might need to see a little more information.

For this, Opsview uses **Log4perl**, which allows us to increase log verbosity levels on the fly. It can take up to 30 seconds before changes are propagated.

For any process that is reported in `opsviewd.log`, simply edit `/usr/local/nagios/etc/Log4perl.conf` and set the log level for the service you want. This is done by using the following code:

```
log4perl.logger.import_ndologsd=DEBUG
log4perl.logger.import_perfdatarrd=DEBUG
```

Once done, simply save the file and check the log file to see more data being generated (remember to turn off debugging once done).

For any issues with the Opsview Web interface, we can again use Log4perl to increase log levels. For this, simply edit the file `/usr/local/opsview-web/etc/Log4perl.conf` and increase the levels as needed (some examples are provided in the file). Then open the `opsview-web.log` file and check the results.

Common agent issues

From time to time, agents will report problems ranging from configuration mishaps to more complex issues, such as missing libraries. In this section, we will look at some of the most common causes and how to resolve them.

CHECK_NRPE: Error – Could not complete SSL handshake

The `CHECK_NRPE: Error - Could not complete SSL handshake` error is most commonly seen when using old **NRPE** agents in Opsview. By default, Opsview uses NRPE with SSL enabled so all exchanged data is encrypted.

To resolve this issue, simply install the required SSL libraries on the remote host and restart the agent, or replace it with the Opsview-agent.

Another well-known culprit is the **allowed_host** settings on the remote host that does not allow the Opsview server to communicate with the host. To resolve this issue, simply update the remote hosts configuration (usually in `/usr/local/nagios/etc/nrpe.cfg`) and restart the agent.

NRPE: Command '<my command>' not defined

In *Chapter 4*, *Agents, Cloud, and Modules*, we discussed how to add plugins to a remote host. The `NRPE: Command '<my command>' not defined` error tells us that the check we are trying to call has not been defined, as discussed in the same chapter.

To resolve this issue, double check the remote hosts configuration, make the appropriate changes, and restart the agent.

NRPE: Return code of 127 is out of bounds – plugin may be missing

The `NRPE: Return code of 127 is out of bounds - plugin may be missing` error is most commonly caused by incorrect settings in the remote agent or when the plugin is not located where it was defined.

To resolve this issue, double check the remote host configuration and make sure the plugin is located where our command definition states it is. Also, make sure it is executable by the user Nagios.

NRPE: Return code of 255 is out of bounds

NRPE uses system return codes to determine the state (OK, CRITICAL, and so on). Sometimes plugins run into issues and return a system exit code that is not known to NRPE. This will cause the NRPE: Return code of 255 is out of bounds error

In most cases, this is caused by the plugin not having sufficient privileges to run correctly. Verify this by running the plugin on the command-line as the user Nagios and then execute echo $? to see the return code.

Summary

In this chapter, we have seen some great tools that come with Opsview. We have looked at how we can run some debugging and check the logs for information. We have also covered some of the most common problems that we face while using agents.

In the next chapter, we will look at how we can design our monitoring environment to suit our needs, some of the things we need to consider, and some ideas on how to improve our setup to be more effective.

7
Designing a Monitoring Environment

So far, we have focused on how to use Opsview, plugins, agents, and so on. Using these building blocks, we can now look at how we could use these to set up a monitoring environment suited to our organization.

By adding hosts, assigning templates, creating groups, and so on, we will get the basics sorted; but if we really want an effective system, we need to consider how we want our monitoring to operate within our company and how we want our users to work with Opsview to get the best out of it.

Scaling

Now that we have a clear understanding of what Opsview can do, we also need to look at how we can deploy our environment and best scale our setup.

Opsview can be run both on physical hardware as well as on a virtualized environment. For a typical system, the following specifications that can monitor about 300 to 400 hosts are required:

- Multi-core CPU (64-bit)
- 4 GB RAM
- 80 GB of local storage

Now, the number of hosts you can monitor on the given specifications largely depends on how we monitor them. The following is a rule of thumb for the given specifications:

- Average of 10 service checks per host
- 5-minute interval per service check (on an average)
- Majority of service checks against remote agents (NRPE/SNMP)
- Majority of hosts on the same network segment (same location)
- Systems are relatively stable with minor state changes

As these numbers are just guidelines, make sure you keep track of the memory and CPU usage on your Opsview system and add more if needed (Opsview does automatically monitor all these on your Opsview system by default).

Another aspect that should be considered in terms of system performance is tuning the databases that Opsview uses. Tuning MySQL can greatly reduce overhead on your system.

Please refer to the Opsview documentation at `http://docs.opsview.com/doku.php?id=opsview-core:mysql#mysql_performance_tuning` for more information on MySQL tuning.

Deployments

Depending on your hardware, Opsview Core can scale quite nicely to a large system, but what if we have two (or more) data centers? In that case, we can deploy multiple Opsview Core systems.

Using the tools discussed in *Chapter 2, Basic Configuration*, or *Chapter 3, Advanced Configuration*, we can import/export any templates and plugins required to keep systems in sync.

For its Pro and Enterprise solutions, Opsview does offer a distributed setup where we run a single Opsview instance and deploy remote slaves, which we will discuss in *Chapter 10, Opsview Enterprise Features*.

Monitoring concepts

Before we look at some monitoring concepts, I would like you to carefully consider the following statement:

 Monitoring should be aimed at preventing and predicting problems, not just detecting problems.

As systems become more and more complex and more interconnected with other systems, we need an equally sophisticated monitoring solution. This depends on many factors: are we using multi-homed servers, do we have different data centers, how do users connect to our systems and applications, and how do they use them.

We also need to consider how we want to measure our own effectiveness in terms of whether we are monitoring the right things or have we missed a vital piece of information that could have prevented a major outage.

Make sure that after each incident, you review your monitoring to verify whether you are running the right checks and add new checks if needed. If your company does an after-action review (or Root Cause Analyses), information from the monitoring system can be invaluable for these analyses.

Once analyzed, recommendations can then be placed into the monitoring solution to prevent similar incidents from occurring in the future. Another very important thing to look out for is false positives. They will undermine the trust placed in the monitoring system. If a check does not warrant any action, it should not send out alerts.

How to measure availability and performance

So how do we determine when something is available, and what role does performance play in availability? The answer is that they are linked simply because performance plays a major part in making something available.

Let's consider a website using Opsview. We measure if we can connect to port 80 using HTTP and get a response from the web server. This response might take up to 30 seconds, but if our corporate website takes 30 seconds to respond, our visitors might have already lost interest.

Setting up the correct availability checks revolves around getting as much information as possible from your end users and application administrators on how the application works. Here's a list of the most common information needed:

- Names of processes that should be running on the system
- Connection information (how do users connect)
- Interface information (for multi-homed systems)
- Relation to other systems (do we depend on another system for operations)
- Expected performance for the user interface (**thresholds**)

Once this information is in, you can create an overview (document) of checks to determine the system on which you will be running the checks, which thresholds are going to be applied, and which dependencies exist. From this overview of checks, try to determine which check best represents the application in terms of availability. The service check that has the closest matches to the end users' experience is a good starting point.

As an application might span various systems, you might have multiple availability checks for various parts of the system. Try to create a single document per host to keep track (or register this in a wiki), so whenever a system is updated, you can immediately see which other systems should also be updated.

Here is an example showing two hosts with two checks each. This is just a basic example; a fully populated documentation will contain much more information.

Host name	Service check
Web server	check_http -H $HOSTADDRESS$
Web server	check_procs -C httpd
Database server	check_tcp -H $HOSTADDRESS$ -p 3306
Database server	check_procs -C mysqld

Dependencies

Apply dependencies where possible. In the previous example, making `check_http` depend on `check_procs` will, for instance, allow us to detect a firewall blocking HTTP traffic, thus speeding up the process of finding the root cause of our issue.

Make sure to document all dependencies; see the *Using dependencies* section in *Chapter 2, Basic Configuration*, for more information.

Thresholds

Most plugins support the use of thresholds, allowing us to make sure we are warned when the performance is degrading (for instance, a response taking more than 15 seconds from our web server).

Thresholds should always be based on requirements from the end user and application administrators and should be broken down into a warning (for acceptable conditions) and a critical (unusable/unavailable). In both the cases, we require to take action; if not, do not apply the threshold (setting only a critical threshold, for instance, is perfectly fine).

When we look in terms of preventing issues from arising, setting the correct thresholds is very important. So review the thresholds on a regular basis and make sure you have documented appropriate actions (either manually or using event handlers) to be taken when they occur. See `http://docs.opsview.com/doku.php?id=opsview-core:usingeventhandlers` for more information on using event handlers.

Update the documentation with any of the thresholds that should be applied as shown here:

Host name	Service check	Threshold
Web server	check_http -H $HOSTADDRESS$	-w 20 -c 30
Web server	check_procs -C httpd	-w 5:50 -c 0:100
Database server	check_tcp -H $HOSTADDRESS$ -p 3306	-w 10 -c 20
Database server	check_procs -C mysqld	-c 0

Keywords

Creating keywords, as discussed in the *Creating and using keywords* section in *Chapter 3, Advanced Configuration*, will allow us to group together all the information (checks and hosts) that are part of our corporate website infrastructure. So, if we have two hosts belonging to the same system, a web server and a database server, we can tag both hosts with our **website** keyword and create a view for the entire system.

Another option is to tag only the service checks associated with the website, allowing a more focused view. Use the information gathered previously to determine what the best use of a keyword would be and which checks and hosts should be tagged.

Add any keywords you decide on using for the information or documentation, creating a nice overview of all the items related to the system at one place. Also keep in mind that we can use our keywords for notifications.

Here is an example of a keyword table that we can use with our previous example:

Keyword	Hostname	Service check
website	Web server	check_http
website	Database server	check_tcp
database	Database server	check_tcp, check_procs

Using notifications

Another thing we need to consider is how we should use notifications. We have already seen how to set up notifications in the *Configuration notifications* section in *Chapter 3, Advanced Configuration*, but now we need to look at how to use them so that they are most effective.

Most people will have the urge to enable as many notifications as possible but this might be counterproductive instead (especially when thresholds are not yet configured correctly). So carefully consider when to enable and when to disable notifications for a specific service.

Notifications are usually deployed to inform administrators that something has gone wrong and their attention is required, but we can also deploy notifications in a more organization-oriented manner. We could, for instance, use notifications to inform our helpdesk that our corporate website is less responsive and that calls from customers aren't coming in.

For this, we can again turn to our service check (and keyword) overview and determine which checks should be used to notify specific users or groups of users. Make sure to add this information to your documentation so that later on it can be reviewed and updated when new requirements come up, for instance.

Here is an example showing which groups should receive notifications (based on keywords):

Notification (keyword)	Group
website	Helpdesk, web and database administrators
database	Web and database administrators

Notifications can ease the task of informing multiple groups of any situation that might affect their work area.

Multi-homed environments

Monitoring a multi-homed environment brings some additional challenges. We have already seen how we can manage these kinds of environments using Opsview in the *Monitoring multi-homed hosts* section in *Chapter 3, Advanced Configuration*.

While creating host templates for your multi-homed environment, it is important to always use the same configuration for your hosts. Make a visual representation of how checks are executed and against which interface to clarify this if needed.

A simple example is the situation where we have a management network (used to perform maintenance on the host) and a production network (where users can connect to the server). We can then use the management network (defined as $ADDRESS1$) to perform checks on basic metrics like CPU load, memory, disk usage, and running processes, while we use the production network (defined as $ADDRESS2$) to verify if the web server is reachable.

If we then apply the same configuration to all our multi-homed hosts, we can use $ADDRESS1$ and $ADDRESS2$ throughout all our checks (and host templates) without fear of running checks against the wrong interface.

Again, keep track of this in the overview you created (or on your wiki), so everyone is aware of how a typical system is deployed within Opsview, as shown here:

Host	Interface	Network segment
Web server	eth0	Internet facing
Web server	eth1	Management network

Network outages

Although we have already discussed the use of parenting in the *Using parenting for network outage detection* section in *Chapter 3, Advanced Configuration*, it is a vital part of the monitoring environment and, as such, very important when deploying your environment.

When Opsview detects a network outage, it will suppress notifications for any affected host (except the host that was found to have caused the issue). So getting your network correctly represented in Opsview is very important.

As we have seen, adding network devices is fairly straightforward using SNMP, so get your network administrators involved so that you can make full use of parenting (and also help the network team find issues faster). Again, keep track of any parenting information within your overview documentation (as each network device should also be documented, thus getting an impact assessment for a specific network device becomes quite easy).

The following screenshot is a small example of how we could document the parenting information (here, we have added all parents between our web server and our Opsview system).

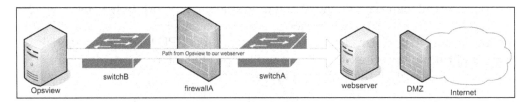

Real path monitoring

We have already mentioned multi-homed hosts, complex systems and networks, and the challenges they give us in terms of monitoring. There is one thing we have not covered yet.

Systems become more and more interconnected, and we need a valid way of monitoring this kind of interaction. Now, real path monitoring is simply the concept of monitoring connections between systems from the system that initiates the connection.

A simple example would be a network split into a **DMZ (Demilitarized Zone)** where our web server resides and a production network where our database server and Opsview server reside. A firewall is used to connect the DMZ to our production network, and our web server uses the database for production information.

In the next image, we will see that Opsview monitors both systems (including the firewall that is not shown), but it will not be able to detect when (due to a configuration issue on the firewall, for instance) the database is unavailable for the web server (see the network shown on the left).

For Opsview to monitor the systems, we must add a service check to our web server that will monitor the real path taken from the web server to the database server (see the network shown on the right).

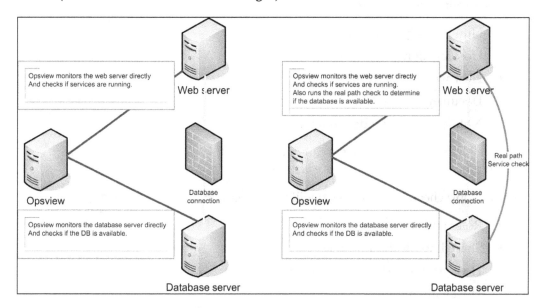

Using real-path monitoring based on the information overview, we can greatly increase the effectiveness of our monitoring setup as we will now be able to detect any failures between systems and pinpoint the root cause more accurately.

Make sure that any real path check is added to your documentation, as shown here:

Host	Service check	Remote host	Remote service
Web server	check_tcp	Database server	MySQL on port 3306

Using these types of checks will greatly enhance the efficiency of your monitoring setup, allowing it to quickly pinpoint where the issues are located and need attention.

Running your environment

Running a well-deployed and well-equipped monitoring system takes some time and effort to set up, and even then, we will keep on improving and tuning it continuously, and as we have seen, there are quite some considerations to be made.

Here's a short recap (a checklist , you could say) on how we can best create our environment.

First, determine the following items:

- Number of hosts (scaling)
- Host locations (deployments)
- How we monitor (multi-homed)
- Documentation (wiki)
- Notifications (who do we wish to notify)

Once we have these numbers, we can deploy our Opsview systems and start building the required infrastructure within Opsview.

Here's a short checklist of items we will need to cover:

- Roles and contacts
- Shared notification profiles
- Host groups and host group hierarchy
- Host templates

Depending on your requirements, you will need to make some adjustments, but any time you put in now will repay you later on (that is, once the configuration is done) and adding new hosts and services will become very easy.

Summary

As we have seen, simply deploying a system will not give us the results we want. Since Opsview can be adapted to handle any situation, having a clear strategy on how you want to use Opsview is essential, as we have discussed in this chapter.

Taking time to consider how you deploy will help you in getting the most out of your monitoring system.

In the next chapter, we will look at how we can upgrade our Opsview Core system to an Opsview Pro or Opsview Enterprise version, and how we can add additional modules to our Pro or Enterprise edition to further enhance the capabilities.

8
Upgrading to Opsview Pro or Opsview Enterprise

So far, we have been looking at Opsview Core, the open source edition from Opsview, and as we have seen, it plays a pivotal role in monitoring our entire IT environment.

As the importance of good monitoring increases, so do the requirements for the monitoring solution, and so Opsview also offers two subscription-based, fully supported systems called Opsview Pro and Opsview Enterprise.

These two products not only contain more functionality (in the form of modules) but also are fully supported through the Opsview helpdesk, and customers can even weigh in on new feature requests.

Why upgrade?

So why would you want to upgrade to Pro or Enterprise? Well, in the next chapters, we will be looking at the various modules included in each version, but here is a short list showing some of the advantages Opsview Pro and Enterprise have over Opsview Core:

- Dashboards allowing the full visualization of your IT environment
- Distributed monitoring for multiple data centers from a single Opsview instance
- Reporting capabilities (SLA, availability, and performance reports) in various formats including PDF and spreadsheet

- Autodiscovery of hosts (including virtual hosts)
- SNMP Trap support for any device capable of sending SNMP traps
- Tenancy that allows multiple customers to use a single Opsview instance without knowing anything about other tenants using the same system

Upgrading or fresh install

If you have been running Opsview Core already and have decided to move to Opsview Pro or Enterprise, upgrading is of course the most suitable path to take.

There are a number of steps involved in upgrading, which we will discuss here (if you have chosen a fresh install, you can skip the *Dashboard* section and continue from *Prerequisites*).

Dashboard

One of the major differences between Core and Pro/Enterprise is the dashboard system, which due to all its offerings will be discussed in a separate chapter (*Chapter 12, Opsview Dashboards*).

When upgrading, simply make a database password entry in the `opsview.conf` configuration file placed under `/usr/local/nagios/etc` as shown here:

```
$dashboard_dbpasswd = "changeme";
```

Then, create an empty database using the password as set in the configuration file (depending on your MySQL setup, these commands might vary a bit).

```
mysql -u root -p<MYSQL ROOT PASSWORD>
CREATE DATABASE IF NOT EXISTS dashboard;
GRANT ALL ON dashboard.* TO dashboard@localhost IDENTIFIED BY
  'changeme' WITH GRANT OPTION;
GRANT ALL ON dashboard.* TO dashboard@'%' IDENTIFIED BY 'changeme'
  WITH GRANT OPTION;
```

The database will be populated during the installation of the Opsview packages.

Prerequisites

If this is a fresh install, please refer to the *Prerequisites* section of *Chapter 1, Opsview Core Basics*, for the additional steps needed to install Opsview.

Entitlement

First, make sure you have received your entitlement key and entitlement ID. The entitlement key is used for access to the Opsview repositories, where the packages are located and the entitlement ID is used to activate your system. You might either have received this through e-mail or you can look it up on the customer portal located at `http://support.opsview.com`.

Depending on your operating system, you will now need to change your repository settings to include the key. Here's an example for a Debian-based Squeeze system using an example key:

```
deb https://downloads.opsview.com/k/
  5bbd5667b498d81af9c2311d871858b26fe0024b/opsview-commercial/
  latest/apt squeeze main
```

More examples for other operating systems can be found at `http://docs.opsview.com/doku.php?id=repositories`.

Once you have configured the repository, simply update your package manager (use the command `apt-get update` if running Debian/Ubuntu) and install the new packages (use the `apt-get install opsview` command if running Debian/Ubuntu).

When the installation is done, go to Opsview's web frontend (`http://your-opsview-system:3000`) to activate your product.

Activating Opsview Pro or Enterprise

After installing, we go to the web frontend of Opsview. We will need to enter our entitlement ID that you should have received together with your entitlement key (which we used to configure the repositories).

Simply enter your ID in the following screen and click on **Submit**:

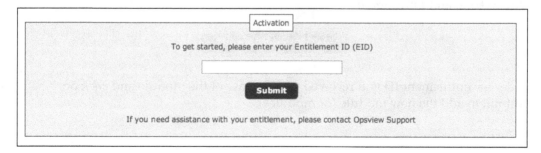

To activate the entitlement, your Opsview system needs to have access to the Internet. If this is not available, you can manually activate your system by following the instructions at `http://docs.opsview.com/doku.php?id=opsview4.4:manual-entitlement-activations` or by contacting the Opsview helpdesk.

You can verify your entitlements by going to **help | About | Your System and Entitlements** in the Opsview web interface, shown in the following screenshot (the screenshot is just an example):

Feature	Status	Expiry Date	Details
Host Monitoring	Enabled	2014-03-08 23:59:59	Limited to 100
Status User Interface	Enabled	2014-03-08 23:59:59	N/A
Dashboard	Enabled	2014-03-08 23:59:59	N/A
Dashboard Multi-Master	Disabled	N/A	N/A
Data Warehouse	Disabled	N/A	N/A
Distributed Monitoring	Disabled	N/A	N/A
Slave Server Clustering	Disabled	N/A	N/A
SNMP Trap Processing	Enabled	2014-03-08 23:59:59	N/A
Reports Module	Disabled	N/A	N/A
Service Desk Connector Module	Disabled	N/A	N/A
Netaudit Module	Disabled	N/A	N/A
NetFlow Module	Disabled	N/A	N/A

Adding additional entitlements

As shown in the previous image, you can add additional modules to your Opsview system and simply click on the **Add an entitlement** button under **help | About | You System and Entitlements**.

Add an entitlement

Enter the entitlement ID you received on purchase of the module and click on **Submit** to add the new module (or modules).

Summary

Upgrading to a fully supported and modular monitoring environment, as we have shown here, is quite easy. For any organization serious about IT monitoring, this is a great and easy step to keep their IT environment in control.

Now that we have seen how easy it is to upgrade (or do a fresh install), we will take a further look at the various modules that come with Opsview Pro and Enterprise or those you can add to the system.

9
Opsview Pro Features

As seen in *Chapter 8, Upgrading to Opsview Pro or Opsview Enterprise*, our new system comes with some additional features that we can use to further enhance our monitoring environment.

In this chapter, we will be looking at three great features that come with each Opsview Pro installation.

We will start off with autodiscovery, followed by SNMP traps, and conclude with multitenancy.

Autodiscovery

The first feature we will look at is the autodiscovery tool that allows you to scan your network for hosts that could be monitored by Opsview.

There are two types of scans available from the feature: a basic network scan and a special VMware scan (more scan types may be added in the future).

Firewalls

If your network is protected (and divided) by firewalls, you might have trouble running scans (or get fewer results than you expected); this is caused by firewalls detecting the scan and marking it as unwanted traffic.

If you experience issues, make sure that you check the firewall and verify that it is allowing traffic from the Opsview server.

Network scan

To start a scan, navigate to **settings | Basic | Auto-Discovery** and click on the **Network Scan** button to bring up the configuration menu for our new scan.

There are two sections that can be used to perform our scan. The first section covers the basics such as a label for our scan, the IP addresses (you can use network statements such as `192.168.1.0/24`), and a number of default settings, as shown in the following screenshot:

The second section (**Detection Mapping**) covers the detection mechanisms which include detection of common network services (such as SMTP, WWW, and so on), agent-based detection, and agentless detection using WMI, SNMP, and VMware vSphere host detection, as shown in the following screenshot:

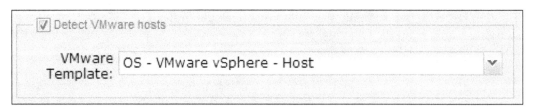

Now, click on **Save** and you will see that a new job is created using our settings, and by clicking on our job, we can start the scan, edit, clone, or delete it.

Depending on the number of IPs to scan and the number of services set up in the detection section scans, an estimated time for completion is shown once you click on **Save**.

Once our job has finished, we can view the results by double-clicking on our job name, and we will be presented with a list of detected hosts and services.

You can edit each host or edit in bulk and then import them into Opsview by selecting the hosts and clicking on **Import into Opsview**. You can then see your new hosts on the **settings | Basic | Hosts** screen.

VMware scan

A VMware scan is a quick way of finding VM guests running in your virtual environment and importing them into Opsview.

Before we can run a VMware scan, there are some requirements we need to look at.

First, we must have the VMware vSphere SDK for Perl installed on our Opsview server (which you can download from the VMware website: `https://my.vmware.com/web/vmware/details?downloadGroup=SDKPERL550&productId=353`).

Next, each VM Guest should be running the VMware tools as we will use these to gather IP information about our guests from our VMware vSphere Hosts.

And finally, we need our VMware hosts that we can scan for using the network scan and enabling the detection mapping for VMware, as shown in the previous section.

The VMware mapping is based on using the vSphere SDK to communicate with the VMware API; so make sure that the Opsview server can communicate with your vSphere servers using HTTPS.

Shown in the following screenshot is an example of a detected VMware vSphere host:

Click on **VMware**, enter the VMware credentials for the host, save it, and click on **VMware scan** from the **Scan management** tab to start a scan for VMs running on this host (or hosts if multiple vSphere hosts were detected).

This uses the same principles as the VMware detection mapping and uses the VMware API to communicate with vSphere.

Additionally, Opsview will automatically set the parent of the detected guests as the VMware host; so, you do not have to manually add the parent.

Once completed, select and import the VMs after which you can view the new hosts from the **settings** | **Basic** | **Hosts** list.

SNMP traps

Most network devices are capable of sending out SNMP traps when certain events occur (this is not restricted to network equipment though).

Using the SNMP trap receiver in Opsview allows you to catch these events and process them in Opsview.

Please note that setting up and using SNMP traps is a complex task, and being familiar with the command line and SNMP tools in general is highly recommended.

Traps received by Opsview are evaluated based on the originating host, and if this host has an SNMP trap service check assigned to it, it will be evaluated based on the rules of the service check (a host can have multiple SNMP trap service checks, and each service check can have multiple rules).

To use SNMP traps in Opsview, we will need to configure our system so that any incoming traps are forwarded to Opsview.

Configuration

Depending on your operating system, you will need to install the SNMPD packages that are required for SNMP traps.

On Debian/Ubuntu-based systems, run `apt-get install snmpd` to install the required packages. Once installed, we need to configure the following items so that we can use device-specific MIBs.

Add the following line to your `snmp.conf` file (file and location might vary depending on the operating system) to add the `/usr/local/nagios/snmp/load` directory (this is the directory where we can add device-specific MIBs to be used with Opsview).

```
mibdirs +/usr/local/nagios/snmp/load
```

Next, we need to set up the trap receiver by adding these lines to the `/etc/default/snmpd` configuration file:

```
TRAPDRUN=yes
TRAPDOPTS='-t -m ALL -M /usr/share/snmp/mibs:/usr/local/nagios/snmp/
load -p
  /var/run/snmptrapd.pid'
SNMPDOPTS='-u nagios -Lsd -Lf /dev/null -p/var/run/snmpd.pid'
```

Now, we need to configure the SNMP trap daemon to forward any events received to Opsview; for this, we edit the `snmptrapd.conf` configuration file and add:

```
traphandle default /usr/local/nagios/bin/snmptrap2nagios
```

And finally, we need to allow the user running Opsview (the nagios user) to be able to restart SNMP and the SNMP trap daemons if we load new MIBs and so on by adding the following line to our `sudoers` file using the `visudo` command:

```
nagios ALL=NOPASSWD: /usr/local/nagios/bin/snmpd reload
```

Once completed, we can now start using the SNMP traps in Opsview.

SNMP trap service check

Opsview Pro does come with a number of predefined SNMP trap service checks and host templates and they will cover the basics, but you can create your own checks with your own rules as we will see here.

Once configured, we can start creating SNMP trap service checks (which is similar to the process discussed in the *Creating service checks* section in *Chapter 2, Basic Configuration*); only, now we will have some additional options, as shown in the following screenshot:

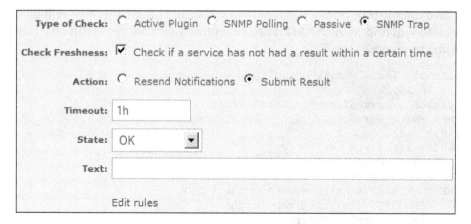

By clicking on the **Edit rules** link at the bottom of the screen, we can edit any rules assigned to this check.

The rules form the basis of the SNMP trap system, and you can create multiple rules within one service check (the processing will stop when a rule that is considered TRUE is found and any subsequent rules are then skipped).

The following screenshot shows an example of a group of rules that will be checked against (taken from the SNMP Trap - Link State service check):

	Name	Rule	Alert Level	Message
🗑	Network link down	"${TRAPNAME}" eq "IF-MIB::linkDown"	CRITICAL	CRITICAL Interface ${V6} has changed state to ${V8}
🗑	Network link up	"${TRAPNAME}" eq "IF-MIB::linkUp"	OK	OK Interface ${V6} has changed state to ${V8}
🗑	Ignore rest	1	Stop	

Exceptions

If for some reason the devices are sending traps that Opsview can't process (due to lack of rules or missing MIBs), they will end up in the **SNMP Trap Exceptions** section located at **settings | Advanced | SNMP Traps**.

From this menu, you can view traps that have failed to match and view debug information that can be used to fix any rules or help in creating rules.

Rules

Making rules for SNMP traps works by using lines, values, and tags to perform matching. So let's have a look at an example SMNP trap to see how we can create rules.

Here's an example trap from a Cisco network device. This information will be similar to what you will find in the **SNMP Trap Exceptions** section. For clarity, we have added line numbers.

```
cisco2611.lon.altinity
192.168.10.20
SNMPv2-MIB::sysUpTime.0 9:16:47:53.80
SNMPv2-MIB::snmpTrapOID.0 IF-MIB::linkUp
IF-MIB::ifIndex.2 2
IF-MIB::ifDescr.2 Serial0/0
IF-MIB::ifType.2 ppp
SNMPv2-SMI::enterprises.9.2.2.1.1.20.2 "PPP LCP Open"
SNMP-COMMUNITY-MIB::snmpTrapAddress.0 192.168.10.20
SNMP-COMMUNITY-MIB::snmpTrapCommunity.0 "public"
SNMPv2-MIB::snmpTrapEnterprise.0 SNMPv2-SMI::enterprises.9.1.186
```

The first two lines are host information and used to map the trap to our host; we can use the remaining lines in our rules using the following macros.

${TRAPNAME} will map to the value snmpTrapOID.0 on the fourth line which in this case is IF-MIB::linkUp.

${Px} will map to the parameter on line x; so, for instance, ${P7} will map to the parameter (ifType) on the seventh line (any trailing numbers such as .2 are ignored).

${Vx} will map to the value on line x, so ${V6} will map to Serial0/0.

You can also directly call the value of an OID by placing it in your rule; so, for instance, ${SNMP-COMMUNITY-MIB::snmpTrapCommunity} will map to public.

Matching

So now that we have seen how we can take the information in our traps and use them, we need to look at how we can match against them.

For this, we can use simple Perl matching mechanisms such as eq or =~ (to do pattern matching).

So, a comparison to check if the SNMP trap community string is set to be used, the string public could be expressed in these different forms:

```
"${V10}" eq "public"
"${SNMP-COMMUNITY-MIB::snmpTrapCommunity}" eq "public"
```

Both statements are the same; the first one is less readable. It might be unwanted if you wish to make a lot of rules and be able to quickly see what each rule does.

We can also combine matches in a single line, for instance, if we wish to check if the community is set to public and the interface reported is of a specific type.

```
"${V10}" eq "public" && "${V7}" eq "ppp"
```

Using the AND (&&) and OR (||) operators, we can create all kinds of combinations allowing for a finely tuned rule set.

Creating rule sets is best done by making good use of the exceptions as they contain the trap in exactly the form in which it will be processed (line, parameters, and so on). So, if you are planning on adding a new type of device and you need to develop new rules, make good use of the various screens.

Multitenancy

In *Chapter 1, Opsview Core Basics*, we discussed the roles and contacts within an Opsview system and how they allow us to define which user can see which part of the system.

But what if each group within your company has its own IT department, or maybe you are a service provider with multiple customers and don't want to set up an Opsview system per customer?

Opsview Pro offers a solution called tenancy for this, and a number of rules dictate how the tenancy works. The rules are as follows:

- The primary role of a tenancy defines the maximum permissions available to all tenants
- Each tenant role can define a subset of permissions based on the primary role
- Each tenant can only see objects that are within their own tenancy
- The primary role cannot be edited by anyone in the tenancy
- Non-tenant users can see within the tenancy if their access allows this

Using tenancies, we can make nicely contained groups for each of our customers and give them full privileges within their tenancy (for instance, they can add their own users and hosts) without them having access to other customers' information.

The biggest difference between tenancy and roles that we discussed earlier is that we can have full admin privileges for a tenant while still keeping the user contained; in regular roles, a full admin will be able to access the entire system.

Creating tenancies

To set up tenancies, we need to create a specific host group (one for each tenancy) that will house the group (you can move host groups around from the **settings | Groups | Host Group Hierarchy** screen).

Next, we create a new role that has the highest possible permissions we want within our tenancy, making sure we assign this role to the host group we created earlier in the **Configuration** tab (in the **Host Groups** section of the tab).

The create role screen in Opsview Pro includes the option to make a new role a primary role as shown in the following screenshot, where we are creating the primary role for CustomerA.

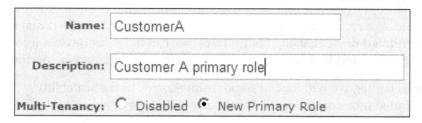

Selecting the **New Primary Role** radio button will remove some possible configuration options that would otherwise clash with the tenancy setup.

Once we have created our primary role, we can either add more roles (you can use the **For Tenant** option to create new roles within the tenancy) or create the tenancy from the **settings | Administration | Multi-Tenancy** screen.

Click on the **Add** icon to create a new tenancy where you can enter the name and description and select the primary role associated with this tenancy (only roles that have the correct privileges are shown; using the **New Primary Role** option makes sure of that), as shown in the following screenshot:

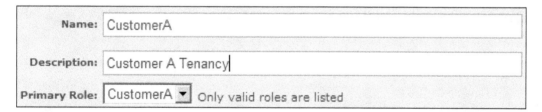

If you have given the primary role the ability to create hosts, host groups, contacts, and roles, your customers will be able to operate with a certain degree of autonomy within your Opsview installation.

Summary

Autodiscovery, SNMP traps, and multitenancy are great features that come with each installation of Opsview Pro.

Using autodiscovery, we can quickly scan our network (or VMware hosts) for new and unmonitored devices; using SNMP traps, we can have our devices inform us in case of trouble; and with tenancies, we can easily create customer specific groups.

In the next chapter, we will look at some features, such as the scalability and distributed monitoring features that come with Opsview Enterprise.

10
Opsview Enterprise Features

In the previous chapter we looked at the features that come with Opsview Pro; in this chapter we will look at features that are part of Opsview Enterprise (note that all the Pro features are by default present in Enterprise).

Opsview Enterprise is geared towards large distributed IT environments and comes with a set of additional features to support this.

Opsview Pro users can use (add) these features to augment the capabilities of their installation as each feature is separately available; this can be very convenient if you only need specific functionality.

Scalability

The scalability feature has two major features: the first is the use of remote database systems, and the second is the use of slaves in our Opsview environment.

The main goal of the feature is to remove workload from our Opsview server by offloading work to other systems.

Opsview databases

Opsview Pro uses four databases and Opsview Enterprise uses five databases. Each database is used for different parts of the system, and to fully understand the scalability feature it is good to understand what each database does.

The main databases are the **Opsview** and **Runtime** databases:

- The Opsview database contains all configuration information (hosts, service checks, and so on)

- The Runtime database contains all information that has been processed (service check results, and so on) for the last seven days

The secondary databases are the **ODW**, **Dashboard**, and **Reports** databases.

- ODW stands for **Opsview Data Warehouse** and contains our historical data (due to the potential size of this, running the ODW on its own system can really help).

- The Dashboard database contains all information and configuration of the dashboards we can create in Opsview, which we will discuss in *Chapter 12, Opsview Dashboards*.

- The Reports database contains all the schedules and report configurations for the reporting module; the data used to generate the reports is pulled from the ODW. This database is only present in an Opsview Enterprise installation unless you have the reporting module for Opsview Pro.

Using remote databases

To use the feature, copy your current database to the new database server (make sure Opsview is not running during the migration to prevent data loss).

Using a full database export will make sure all the necessary information (except access information) is copied. The following command is an example of how we can export our Opsview databases:

```
mysqldump -u root -p --opt --databases opsview runtime odw dashboard
  reports| gzip -c > databases.sql.gz
```

Next we need to edit the `opsview.conf` file, which resides in the `/usr/local/nagios/etc` directory, and add the following statements:

```
$dbhost = "hostname";
$odw_dbhost = "hostname";
$runtime_dbhost = "hostname";
$reports_dbhost = "hostname";
$dashboard_dbhost = "hostname";
```

As you will notice we can set different hostnames for each of the databases (we can also set things such as the database username and password, or even the database name using, for instance, `$odw_dbuser`, `$odw_dbpassword`, and `$odw_db`).

The Runtime database (`$runtime_dbhost`) and the Opsview database (`$dbhost`) must reside on the same system due to joins between these two databases; the other databases can run on their own hosts.

Distributed monitoring

Another feature of the scalability pack is the use of slaves for distributed monitoring.

Using slaves, we can offload the task of running service checks from our Opsview server (which from now on we will call the Opsview **master**) to another system, which is called a slave controlled by the master.

Using slaves, everything is controlled from the master, so all configurations and all results are presented in a single view.

The master and slaves communicate over SSH using a secure tunnel over which data flows between the hosts. This also makes it easy to firewall and makes sure everything is encrypted while in transit.

NRD (**Nagios Result Distributor**) is used by Opsview for sending results of executed service checks from each slave to the master, which the master in turn will process. The NRD mechanism will by default cache results on a slave (up to five minutes, but this is configurable) when the connection with the master is down (the master will always try to reconnect immediately if an SSH tunnel is dropped).

With slaves, we can scale our Opsview Enterprise environment making it suitable to monitor various data centers with thousands of hosts and service checks, all viewable through one interface.

Slaves

In order to add a slave to Opsview, there are some tasks and guidelines, which we must follow.

First the intended slave must be binary compatible with the master, or in other words, must run the same operating system with the same architecture (64-bit or 32-bit).

Create the `nagios` and `nagcmd` groups, and the `nagios` user using the following commands:

```
groupadd nagios
groupadd nagcmd
adduser -g nagios -G nagcmd -d /var/log/nagios -m nagios
```

Next, we need to install the `opsview-slave` package, which will handle any dependency we have on additional software; install this using the package manager of your operating system.

Once the `opsview-slave` package has been installed, set the password for the newly created `nagios` user to something secure using the command `passwd nagios`.

Now we need to allow the `nagios` user to run the installation software it will receive from the master; for this run, `visudo` and add the following line:

```
nagios ALL = NOPASSWD:/usr/local/nagios/bin/install_slave
```

 If you see a line such as `Defaults requiretty`, comment the line as it will break the slave installation.

Next, from our master we need to create an SSH key for our `nagios` user, and send this key to our slave so that it can be used to verify the authenticity of the SSH tunnel.

If your `nagios` user on the master does not yet have an SSH key, simply perform the following steps. If the `nagios` user already has keys, simply copy the public key to the slave.

```
su - nagios
ssh-keygen -t dsa
ssh-copy-id -i .ssh/id_dsa.pub <slave hostname>
```

With the `ssh-copy` command, you will be prompted for the `nagios` user's password, which you set earlier.

Check if SSH works by performing the following task from the master:

```
su - nagios
ssh <slave hostname>
```

If this works, copy two scripts from the master (as the `nagios` user) to the slave by running the following command:

```
scp /usr/local/nagios/installer/check_reqs
  /usr/local/nagios/bin/profile <slave hostname>:
```

Then log in to the slave as the user `nagios` and source the profile followed by running the `check_reqs` program (this will double-check if we have all the required dependencies and performed all the required tasks) as shown:

```
. ./profile
./check_reqs slave
```

If no issues are listed, we need to set up the profile for our `nagios` user; to do so, run the following command:

```
echo "test -f /usr/local/nagios/bin/profile && .
  /usr/local/nagios/bin/profile" >> ~nagios/.profile
chown nagios:nagios ~nagios/.profile
```

The master will—when it takes control of the slave—install the final profile needed, but these steps will make sure everything is set for any future login.

The last task we need to perform is to check that SSH allows TCP port forwarding; this is used by Opsview to map certain ports on the slave, so data flows to the correct process.

In the `sshd_config` file (depending on your operating system it will reside in /etc/ ssh/) check if **AllowTcpForwarding** is set to **yes** (if not, do so and restart SSH).

We have now completed all the pre-installation tasks and can finish configuring our slave server using the Opsview web interface.

Creating a slave

To create a slave in the Opsview web interface, navigate to **settings | Basic | Hosts** and add the slave's information and assign (besides the regular Linux host template) the host template called **Application - Opsview Common** to the host.

Then proceed to **settings | Advanced | Monitoring Servers** and click on the plus sign to create a new monitoring host.

Define a name for your slave system and from the list select the host you wish to assign to become a slave and submit.

As the `nagios` user, we can now test the slave by running the following command on the master:

```
su - nagios
/usr/local/nagios/bin/send2slaves -t <name of the slave system>
```

If everything is okay, run the following command to have the master send the base installation files to our slave:

```
/usr/local/nagios/bin/send2slaves <name of the slave system>
```

Once all the files are copied, log in on the slave server and install the software by running the following commands:

```
su - root
cd /usr/local/nagios/tmp && ./install_slave
```

Once completed, return to the web interface and perform a reload; once this has been done, we can use our slave by moving hosts (either by selecting the new slave in the host-edit screen **monitored by**, or by dragging-and-dropping in the **Monitoring Servers** menu under **settings | Advanced**).

Make sure the slave is configured to monitor itself.

Slave clusters

Opsview Enterprise also has the **slave server cluster** feature, which allows us to create a cluster of slaves where the slaves will perform load balancing of checks and fail over in case of slave failures.

Configuring a cluster uses the same steps as a single slave system we have just seen, but with two additional steps.

The first is that each slave system's nagios user needs to exchange SSH keys with all of its cluster members (which uses the same process as sharing the key from the nagios user on the master).

Now when creating the monitoring server in the web interface instead of selecting just a single slave, we select all of the prepared systems by holding down the *Ctrl* key while selecting, and Opsview will team them up to form a cluster.

You can add a new member to an already existing slave in a similar fashion.

The load is spread across all members by assigning equal amounts of hosts to each slave to monitor. This is calculated at Opsview's reload time.

Additionally, a check called Cluster-node will be created for each node in the cluster, so that every slave can detect if their peer node is running. In a failover scenario, the node will then start actively checking hosts of the failed node.

Note that slave clustering will take over on a single point of failure.

Service desk connectors

Another very useful feature is the service desk connectors, which allows you to link Opsview with your service desk application.

This allows for automatic generation of tickets in your service desk system, and will update (acknowledge) the alert in Opsview with information, such as ticket number, making it easy to track.

Currently the service desk connectors work with the following service desk systems:

- ServiceNow: http://www.servicenow.com/
- RequestTracker: http://www.bestpractical.com/rt/
- JIRA: https://www.atlassian.com/software/jira
- Salesforce Service Cloud: http://www.salesforce.com/service-cloud/overview/
- OTRS: http://www.otrs.com/

Installing the service desk connector

To configure the service desk connectors, we first need to create a database that will hold the notifications using the following commands in MySQL (make sure to change the password shown here as changeme).

```
CREATE DATABASE notifications;
GRANT ALL ON notifications.* TO notifications@'%' IDENTIFIED BY
  'changeme' WITH GRANT OPTION;
```

Next install the opsview-servicedesk-connector package.

For a Debian-based system, we can install the package with the following command:

```
apt-get install opsview-servicedesk-connector
```

Next we need to configure the service desk connector to use our newly created database; for this, simply edit the file notifications.yml located at /etc/opt/opsview/notifications/ and add in the correct credentials.

Now we need to populate the database, which we can do by running the following command:

```
/opt/opsview/notifications/bin/db_notifications db_install --force
```

Connecting your Service Desk System

Now that our database is up and running, we need to configure how we connect to our service desk system.

In the `/etc/opt/opsview/notifications/config.d` directory, there are example files for all supported service desk systems, which you can use (simply remove the `.example` suffix and edit accordingly).

Once done, restart the notification process by running the following command:

```
/etc/init.d/opsview-notifyd restart
```

To use the new connector, simply link the notification script with the following command:

```
ln -s /opt/opsview/notifications/bin/opsview_notifications
  /usr/local/nagios/libexec/notifications/opsview_notifications
```

Then create a new notification method as described in the *Configuring notifications* section in *Chapter 3, Advanced Configuration*.

The **Command** should always be defined as `opsview_notifications`, followed by the name of the service desk system; for instance, for a JIRA service desk connector, we would use `opsview_notifications jira`.

Create a notification profile for this new notification method and assign it to a contact (assign it only once so that tickets are only created once).

Then simply use the regular methods of selection (host groups, service groups, or keywords) to send out notifications, which will be turned into tickets.

Reporting

Monitoring our IT estate will allow us to see if anything is amiss, but users and customers often demand more in terms of SLAs and weekly or monthly reports on how we are achieving the required levels.

Using the reporting module we can provide them with reports on the various measurements ranging from performance reports to availability reports and even top ten reports showing us which parts of a system have the most issues.

In the *Scalability* section, we briefly touched on the databases used by reporting, namely the reports database containing the schedules and settings for the reports, and the ODW, which contains the actual data used to fill the reports.

The ODW is updated on an hourly schedule by importing information from the Runtime database. The ODW has a number of special tables called Summary facts tables, which contain summarized data to make reporting even easier.

To enable the ODW, navigate to **settings | Administration | System Preferences** and click on the **ODW** tab as shown in the following screenshot:

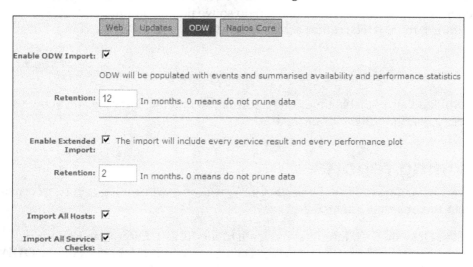

These settings will control what is imported (all hosts and services or just a subsection), how long the data is to be stored before it is removed from the ODW, and if extended data is required.

Next make sure the reporting module is enabled under **settings | Administration | Modules** and that your web server is configured using the apache_proxy.conf file located at /usr/local/nagios/installer/, which will allow for a single sign on in Opsview and the reporting module.

Configuring reporting

To use the reporting module we need to pre-configure our system for the packages.

First we need to create a report group and user depending on your operating system, but for Debian we can achieve this by running the following command as the user root:

```
addgroup --system opsview
```

Next we need to add a user for our group by running the following command:

```
adduser --system --group --home /var/lib/opsview --shell /bin/bash --
  quiet opsview
```

Next simply install the packages required by running the following command:

```
apt-get install opsview-reporting-module opsview-jasper
```

During the installation the reports database will be created and populated.

All data in the ODW is stored in UTC time, but we would naturally like to be able to report using our actual time zone. To do so we need to populate MySQL with time zone information, which can be achieved by running the following commands:

```
whereis zoneinfo
mysql_tzinfo_to_sql /usr/share/zoneinfo | mysql u -root -p mysql
```

This will load all available time zone information into the database and allow us to specify the time zone for our reports.

Running reports

Once we have data imported into the ODW, we can start running reports or schedule them to run at specific times.

From the Opsview web interface, navigate to **modules | Enterprise Reports | Reports**, then from the left menu select **Data Sources**, and right-click on the **ODW** connector shown in the right screen and select **Edit**.

This will bring up the connection information for the ODW allowing you to enter the credentials for the ODW and the URL (if the ODW is on another server).

Nearly all reports use keywords, which we discussed in the *Creating and using keywords* section in *Chapter 3, Advanced Configuration*.

As we have previously discussed using keywords, we can simply create a single view for an application or service (running various programs on various systems); so using them for reporting will make sure all the relevant information for any application or service will be included in the reports.

Types of reports

Opsview comes with a number of predefined reports (and you can of course create your own reports).

All reports use roughly the same input, namely the keyword, a description, an end date, a logo (default reports use the Opsview logo, but you can replace this with your own company logo), and a time zone.

To add your own logo, navigate to the **Images** folder (in the left-hand menu), and then to **Add Resource | Image**, select the image you want, and click on **Next** to give it a name and description before uploading it (reference it as `/images/myimage` in the **Logo** field)

Included here are some of the types of reports that are most commonly used.

Availability

The availability reports will calculate the percentage of time our services were considered to be available.

Using the specific hours version, you can define between which hours and which days (for instance, only during opening hours of the service desk) the results should be used.

The service-level reports also allow us to specify an SLA target in percentages, which will compare each service against our SLA for compliance (do make sure you are running the correct checks for this and if possible, agree on the check(s) with your customer).

Events

The events reports simply create an overview of what happened at what time and can be a great help when analyzing outages and problems.

Combined

The combined reports typically combine availability reports with event reports giving you a great view of not only how much time a service was unavailable, but also shows when and with which events this occurred.

Summary

Opsview Enterprise comes with a lot of additional and great features as we have seen here.

Each of these features can also be used in combination with Opsview Pro to augment your installation.

In the next chapter we will be looking at another set of features Opsview offers to further enhance your Opsview Pro or Opsview Enterprise installation.

11
Additional Modules

In the last two chapters we discussed the modules that come directly with each installation of either Opsview Pro or Opsview Enterprise.

In this chapter we will look at some of the additional modules Opsview offers to further enhance our Opsview installations.

We will also look at some of the reasons why one should choose Opsview Pro or Opsview Enterprise.

The multi-master module

The first of the modules available is the **multi-master** module.

This module allows us to use the Opsview dashboard to view information from another Opsview master (the complete dashboard functionality will be discussed in *Chapter 12, Opsview Dashboards*).

So if you are running multiple masters in, for instance, Europe and America, you can simply use the closest master to access information from the other master in a dashboard.

To use this feature, go to the **Dashboard** menu and on the left you will see the **Multi Masters** button as shown in the following screenshot:

Click on the **Multi Masters** button to bring up the list of masters available; you can also add new masters here by entering their URL and credentials.

Once added, you can now select from which master information should be drawn when you add a dashlet to a dashboard.

The primary master will instruct the client's browser to connect to the secondary master, so no additional connectivity between the two masters is required.

The Network Analyzer module

The Network Analyzer module integrates the **NetAudit** and **NetFlow** modules into your Opsview system.

The NetAudit module

The NetAudit module integrates the well known **RANCID** network configuration management tool with Opsview.

For more information on RANCID, go to http://www.shrubbery.net/rancid/.

If you are running a distributed setup with slaves, you can run NetAudit in a distributed setup to match this. This will turn your slaves into collectors and use the master as the main repository.

To use NetAudit, we must first install the messaging service, which will be used to communicate between our collectors (slaves) and our master.

For this, we need to install the `opsview-activemq` and `opsview-activemq-scripts` packages using our package manager on each of the servers to be used by NetAudit.

Once done, edit the `activemq.xml` file residing at `/opt/opsview/activemq/conf/` on each server to set up the correct connections; for a master we only need to set `transportConnectors` as shown in the following code:

```
<transportConnectors>
  <transportConnector name="openwire" uri="tcp://localhost:4125"/>
  <transportConnector name="stomp" uri="stomp://localhost:61613"/>
</transportConnectors>
```

For a slave server (which will send up the data to the master), we need to edit the settings as shown in the following code:

```
<transportConnectors>
  <!-- stomp is required for any client processes on this server
    to connect to, e.g. file2activemq -->
  <transportConnector name="stomp" uri="stomp://localhost:61613"/>
</transportConnectors>
<networkConnectors>
  <!-- localhost:4125 is connection to upstream opsview master if
    this is an opsview slave -->
  <networkConnector name="master"
    uri="static://(tcp://localhost:4125)" duplex="true"
      networkTTL="2"/>
</networkConnectors>
```

Once done, we can now install the NetAudit module on the master by installing the `opsview-rancid` and `opsview-rancid-master` packages.

On our collectors, the `opsview-perl` and `opsview-rancid-collector` packages should be installed (you can run a collector on a server that is not a slave of Opsview).

Next, enable the NetAudit module by navigating to **settings | Administration | Modules** and if needed, edit the `apache_proxy.conf` file to allow the web server access to the SVN repository (see the *Reporting* section in *Chapter 10, Opsview Enterprise Features*, for more information on the `apache_proxy.conf` file).

Once done, you can configure each host you want to add by navigating to **settings** | **Basic** | **Hosts** and edit the host by clicking on the **RANCID** tab and entering the required credentials as shown in the following screenshot:

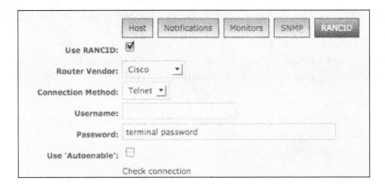

For each host, select the correct vendor and keep in mind that the credentials required might differ from one vendor to the next; for instance, Cisco devices often need a second password (also known as the enable password).

Once done, you can view the collected configurations by navigating to **modules** | **RANCID**.

From **settings** | **Administration** | **System Preferences** on the **RANCID** tab, you can set an e-mail address that will receive notifications when configuration changes have occurred.

The NetFlow module

NetFlow is an industry standard for collecting IP traffic information for traffic monitoring.

Using NetFlow information in Opsview gives us the possibility to view what is happening on our network at a protocol level.

This way we can see not only various types of traffic (HTTP, SMTP, and so on), but also how much bandwidth they consume, which systems are receiving the most traffic, and which systems are sending/generating the most traffic.

To set up NetFlow, we first need to define the collectors (servers which will be receiving NetFlow information) and then we need to define the sources (hosts that will send us NetFlow information).

Configuring NetFlow

From **settings** | **Advanced** | **NetFlow Collectors**, you can select which systems will receive information; this must be either the Opsview master or a slave server (if you have a distributed setup).

From the same page, we can configure the NetFlow settings, such as retention periods (as data can quickly accumulate) as shown in the following screenshot; the settings page also gives a good indication of required storage for the given period.

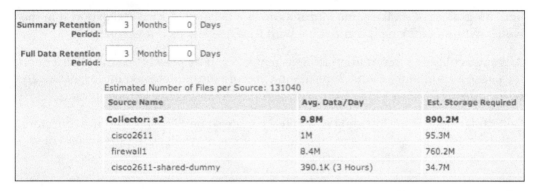

Make sure you assign the host template **Application - Opsview NetFlow Common** to each slave or master you have added as a collector and assign the **Application - Opsview NetFlow Master** template to your master to monitor the various processes involved in NetFlow collection.

Then, click on the **Total sources** link in **settings** | **Advanced** | **NetFlow Collectors** to add an existing host in Opsview as a source.

Next, you must configure your device to send the NetFlow information to Opsview, the configuration of which depends on your specific type of network device; so get the network administrators involved in configuring the network devices you want to collect NetFlow information from (or have them provide suitable devices).

If your network devices do not support NetFlow, you can use the **fprobe** tool for Linux servers and the **nProbe** program for Windows servers to collect NetFlow information (or maybe even run both to get as much information out of your network as possible).

For more information on installing and using fprobe, please visit `http://sourceforge.net/projects/fprobe/`.

For more information on nProbe, visit `http://www.ntop.org/products/nprobe/`.

Both programs collect the same information as a network device and export it in the NetFlow format making it compatible with the Opsview NetFlow collector.

Although collecting information from as many points as possible sounds like a good idea, take a good look at what information you are most interested in (for instance, traffic in your DMZ or traffic from within your network going to the Internet).

Collecting a lot of NetFlow data will take up quite some disk space on the collectors and the master, so make sure to take this into account when sizing the system or when adding new NetFlow sources.

Viewing NetFlow information

Once our system has collected the NetFlow information, we can view this information from the dashboard by clicking on the **Dashboards** link in the web interface.

Here we can create a new dashboard for our NetFlow information.

Click on the plus sign in the main screen to create a new dashboard and click on **NetFlow** in the menu on the left to bring up the various dashlets we can use.

The source dashlets (**Sources Summary** and **Sources History**) will show how much traffic has been seen by the various sources (**Sources Summary**) and how this traffic has been over a time period (**Sources History**) where you can zoom in to get a more granular view.

The **Top 10** dashlets screen gives the possibility to view the 10 highest-ranking transmitters, receivers, or transfers in our network; shown in the following screenshot are the top 10 transfers in our network:

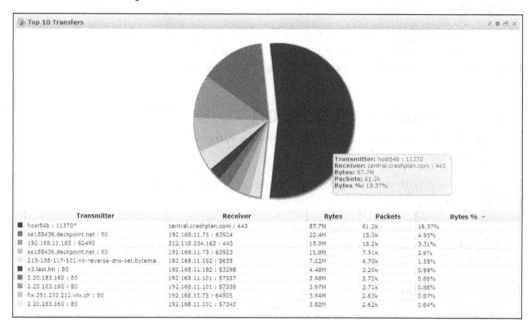

As you can see, this information can be of great value when looking into performance issues on your network or when you are analyzing unresponsive systems (which might be flooded by traffic).

The various other dashlets allow you to build more dashboards where you can use each to analyze your network and IT estate at a whole new level.

NetFlow and tenancy

As NetFlow contains huge amounts of information about traffic flowing through a network, it is only available to non tenancy users.

If a user is part of a tenancy, he or she will not be able to use the NetFlow dashboards as this might expose information about other tenants.

Opsview Pro versus Opsview Enterprise

So when should we choose for Opsview Pro and when should we choose for Opsview Enterprise?

This, of course, largely depends on your IT estate and requirements; so let's recap some of the information we already discussed and add in some numbers to get a better sense of which edition best suits your IT environment.

The Opsview Pro edition

The Opsview Pro edition is suited for IT estates ranging from about 50 hosts up to 200 hosts.

It comes default with dashboards, auto discovery, additional Opspacks, and SNMP traps.

You can further extend the capabilities of Opsview Pro with the Reports module, allowing you to create all kinds of reports and the Scalability module (making it suitable for single or multisite deployments.)

For more information on the subscription plans for Opsview Pro, please visit `http://www.opsview.com/solutions/pro/select-plan`.

To view the various additional modules available for Opsview Pro, visit `http://www.opsview.com/solutions/pro/extend`.

The Opsview Enterprise edition

The Opsview Enterprise edition is suited for IT Enterprise estates ranging from about 200 hosts and more to provide support for multiple data centers housing thousands of hosts and devices.

It not only comes default with all the features of Opsview Pro but also includes the Scalability module, the Reports module, slave server clustering, and service desk connectors.

You can further extend the capabilities of Opsview Enterprise with the multi-master module, the Network Analyzer (NetFlow and NetAudit) module, a test module, and a Sandbox module.

The test module allows you to run an additional Opsview Enterprise (with the same features) for your test network, allowing you to maintain a separation between test and production.

The Sandbox module allows you to run an additional Opsview server with all the features but limited to 100 hosts and is mainly intended for acceptance testing, upgrades, and testing new plugins.

For more information on the subscription plans offered for Opsview Enterprise, please visit `http://www.opsview.com/solutions/enterprise/subscription-plans`.

The Opsview MSP edition

The last of the Opsview editions is the Managed Service Provider version, which has all the features of Opsview Enterprise, but it has an elastic licensing model based on the peak number of hosts you monitor per quarter.

So if you are seeing a high fluctuation in the number of hosts you are monitoring on a quarterly basis, then Opsview MSP will grow (or shrink) with you.

For more information on Opsview MSP, visit `http://www.opsview.com/solutions/msp`.

Summary

In this chapter we looked at some of the additional modules available for Opsview and looked at the differences between the Opsview editions. As Opsview keeps on developing its products, new modules may be added in the future.

In the next chapter we will have a look at the dashboards that come with the Opsview Pro or Opsview Enterprise editions that allow you to create some dazzling visualizations of your IT estate.

12
Opsview Dashboards

One of the most eye-catching features of Opsview is most definitely the dashboards.

Visualization can not only play a very important role in monitoring, but can also help as an aide to show users (or managers) how things are operating in a compelling way.

In *Chapter 11, Additional Modules*, we already had a look at the NetFlow module and a quick look at one of the dashboard dashlets; in this chapter we will show another dashlet available for NetFlow.

We will also look at how we can use the various other dashlets to create overviews that suit the needs and requirements of our users and customers.

We will discuss each dashlet and its intended use, and if you have an Opsview installation running, feel free to look at each dashlet and its options during the process.

Getting started with dashboards

On the web interface click on **Dashboards** to be taken to the dashboard view, which will be empty except for the various menus on the left-hand side of the screen.

To create a dashboard, click on the plus sign in the main area and select what kind of dashboard you wish to create by selecting the number of columns as shown in the following screenshot:

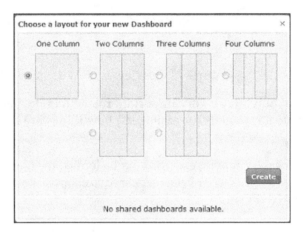

Notice the shared dashboard statement at the bottom; once we have created a new dashboard, we can share this with other users who can then select our dashboard instead of creating their own dashboard (we will look at sharing in *The sharing option* section).

Once it is created, double click on the name of the dashboard to edit it as shown in the following screenshot:

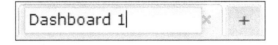

Then, drag-and-drop the dashlets from the menus on the left on to your dashboard.

Each dashlet that you place on a dashboard is configurable, and to access the configuration click on the cog symbol in the header of each dashlet; shown in the following screenshot is the header from one of the business dashlets with the configuration cog visible on the right-hand side.

Business dashboards

The first set of dashlets that come with Opsview are those used by business dashboards.

We have six business dashlets at our disposal to help us visualize information gathered by Opsview to create overviews.

Business dashboards, in general, give a good, high-level overview of various business processes.

The Process Map dashlet

The first dashlet is the **Process Map** dashlet, which allows us to take an image (for instance, the graphical representation of our network or an application) and place various icons on this image; these icons can display information of state, thresholds, and so on.

Using a **Process Map** dashlet with, for instance, a map of an application showing all the relevant information and services, really brings to life an environment.

Here is a very basic example of three systems and their interaction (amount and direction of traffic flowing between the hosts); using more detailed images and more icons (the following screenshot just uses two of the five available icons), you can make fantastically detailed views of your IT environment (we will see another example later on).

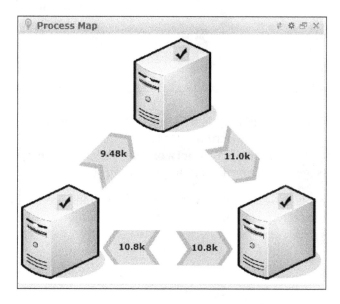

The keyword dashlets

There are three dashlets that use **keywords** to display information, and each dashlet allows us to select the keywords we wish to display (note that this depends on the keywords you are authorized to use in your access profile).

Each dashlet gives a different view of the keywords and the states associated with them, so some might prefer the **Keyword list** view, while others might prefer the **Keyword Tree Map** or **Keyword Cells** view.

Shown in the following screenshot is an example of the **Keyword Tree Map** view; the size of each area depends on the number of checks running within that area (the more the checks, the bigger the area).

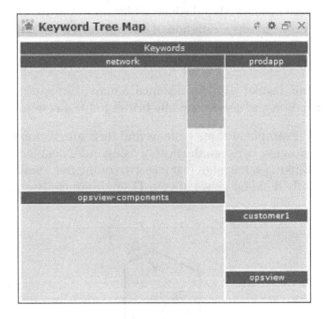

Let's quickly look at what this view is telling us: well; for one, the **customer1**, **opsview**, **prodapp**, and **opsview-components** keywords are all healthy, but apparently something is wrong in our **network** keyword as we have both a critical and warning message (the majority is doing fine though).

As you can see, this is a high-level view well suited for managers who want a global overview, while the technical teams can use this to see which areas they need to focus on.

The performance dashlets

We have two performance dashlets at our disposal, the **Performance Gauge** and **Performance Graph** dashlets.

The gauge allows us to select multiple services on various hosts, and once selected, we can set various thresholds to this selection and apply a scale. This way we can create a single gauge that shows us how a specific service (or services) is performing across one or more servers.

The graph allows us to display one or more performance metrics (from one or more hosts) in a single graph, giving us various options to configure such as the type of graph and the duration that should be shown.

The following is an example of the response time in the last hour for four different web servers in one **Performance Graph**.

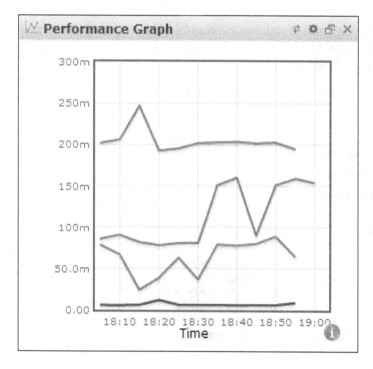

Technical dashboards

Technical dashboards are aimed at supporting technical staff and offer a more low-level view of your IT environment.

There are 10 dashlets available and each dashlet has its own specific use within the dashboards.

The Network Map dashlet

The **Network Map** dashlet will simply generate a view of the network, using the parenting information from Opsview.

You can apply various filters to the map; so, for instance, you can view the network starting at a specific host and showing only those hosts that are the children of this host.

Filters can also be applied to limit the number of host groups shown, and using the advanced filter you can filter based on the monitoring server (if you have slaves), or show only the hosts that act as parents.

Some of the available filters are shown in the following screenshot:

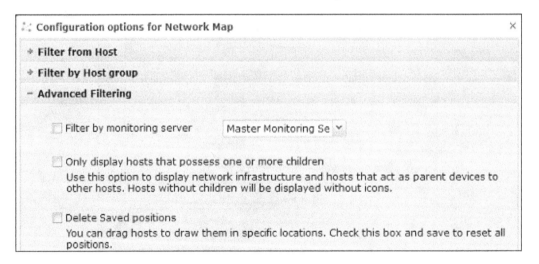

The Metric Pie Chart dashlet

The **Metric Pie Chart** dashlet allows you to create a simple but effective way of comparing values for a service; you can base the pie slices on the host, service, or metric.

Shown in the following screenshot is an example of a **Metric Pie Chart** dashlet based on disk usage on **NAS (Network Attached Storage)**, which shows that each system is consuming roughly the same amount of disk space on our NAS.

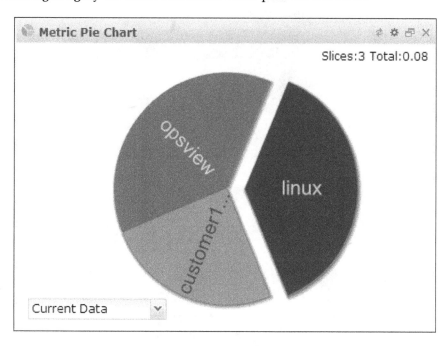

The pie chart offers a great way of comparing metrics and visualizing the system using the greatest amount of slices in percentages.

The host group dashlets

The **Host Group Tree Map** and **Host Group List** dashlets both show a summary of the states and services within the various host groups and allow the use of filters.

The **Host Group Tree Map** dashlet creates a more visual representation of the host groups (using the same principles to draw the areas as the **Keyword Tree Map** dashlet), while the **Host Group List** dashlet will simply create an overview per group.

Shown in the following screenshot is the **Host Group Tree Map** dashlet and the various host groups and their states.

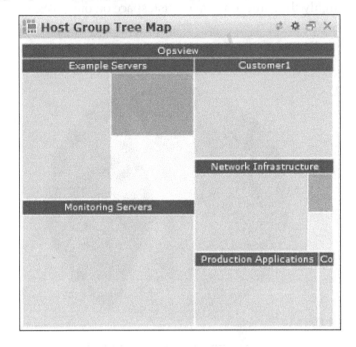

The event dashlets

The **Event Table** and **Event Timeline** dashlets show any registered event within Opsview (for instance, the state changes of a service).

The **Event Table** dashlet will display a simple list with the latest events that occurred at the top of the list, allowing you to quickly go through the latest events.

The **Event Timeline** dashlet shows events in a movable (click-and-drag) timeline view, showing all the events when they occurred.

Shown in the following screenshot is a timeline, and we can see that our host (called **Cisco2960**) was experiencing issues, displayed neatly in our timeline view.

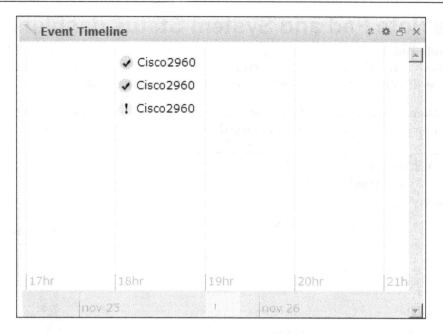

Using the events dashlets can help in tracking down when exactly things happened (and what else occurred around the same time).

The top services dashlets

The top services dashlets are available in two forms.

The **Top Services Issues** dashlet allows us to create a view based on any service and check which hosts have been experiencing issues with that service based on the duration (the longest duration would be the first).

The **Top Services by Metric** dashlet allows us to match against a specific metric (for instance, packet loss) and set some threshold on this metric.

The result is a list of hosts with this service ordered by this threshold, as shown in the following screenshot for the outgoing throughput (in bits per second) of a switch where we have set our own thresholds on the metric, making them change color.

Host	Service	Metric value for throughput_out ▾
Cisco	Interface: FastEthernet0/24	14065884
Cisco	Interface: FastEthernet0/23	356706

The Note Pad and System Status dashlets

The **Note Pad** dashlet allows us to put up a small area where we can make notes (or add short instructions for our co-workers). This is especially useful when sharing a dashboard with multiple users who all need the same instructions.

The **System Status** is a neat dashlet showing the status of our Opsview system. The following screenshot shows both the dashlets side by side:

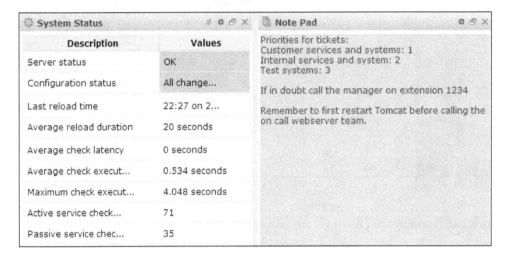

The NetFlow dashboard

Now we already discussed one of the dashlets in the NetFlow dashboard in *The NetFlow module* section in *Chapter 11, Additional Modules,* and we mentioned that NetFlow comes with many more dashlets.

The following screenshot shows an example of the **Top 10 Host Transmitters** showing which host has sent the most amount of data in the last 10 minutes.

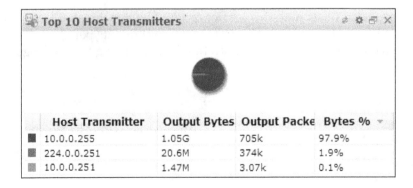

The Top 10 dashlets are really useful in tracking down performance issues in your network. They also give a unique insight into how your network operates and how information (or data) flows through the infrastructure.

Dashboard options

The dashboards themselves also have some options and we already have seen one of them, namely the multimaster, which we discussed in *The multi-master module* section in *Chapter 11, Additional Modules*.

The automatically cycle option

The automatically cycle setting allows us to have a dashboard cycle through at a constant speed, so when we have multiple dashboards, we do not need to keep clicking on each tab to see how things are going. This setting is also great when you have your dashboards up on a big screen where the entire department can see them.

Simply tick the **Automatically cycle through dashboards** box, select the interval from the pull-down menu, and it will immediately start the cycling (as shown in the following screenshot, the dashboards will cycle over 23 seconds).

The sharing option

We already mentioned sharing dashboards at the start of this chapter, so now let's look at how we can configure this.

Simply click on **Share my dashboard** and select the view you wish to share in the following menu, assign it to the role you wish to share it with as shown in the following screenshot, and then click on **Save**.

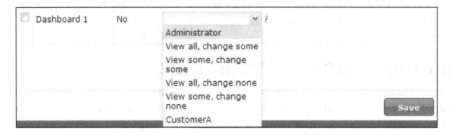

Sharing dashboards is really useful as it allows the more creative users and administrators to create and maintain dashboards and share them with their fellow users. Or as an Opsview administrator, you can simply create and maintain dashboards for your users and customers.

Users and dashboards

Although all users have access to dashboards and can create their own dashboards (and share them), being able to support your users in using dashboards can prevent a wild increase of dashboards.

It will also help your users in understanding what monitoring does and how it supports their daily work.

Requirements

So when discussing dashboards with your users, first try to discover if they are looking for a (low-level) technical-based dashboard or a (high-level) business-based dashboard.

Creating some documentation for your users on how to use the various dashlets, including some examples and step-by-step instructions, will greatly benefit the use and adaptation of dashboards as the means of visualizing your IT estate.

Technical dashboards

If your users are a technical team, create a dashboard (or dashboards) that is focused on their areas of expertise (database administrators don't want to know about switches and so on).

Each dashlet allows for some form of filters, thus allowing you to remove unwanted information from the dashboard; for instance, by removing all the services in a specific state using the state filter shown in the following screenshot:

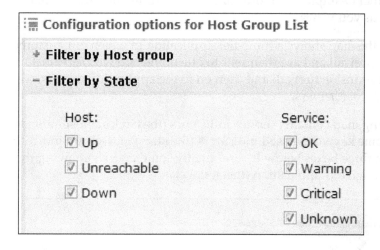

Discuss the various dashlets and their filter options with your users, and if possible, create some examples.

Business dashboards

If, however, your users are looking for business dashboards, carefully examine their requirements and check if appropriate keywords have been used or should be added.

The keyword dashlets allow for a high-level view, not limited by departmental boundaries but spanning the entire IT estate.

As mentioned in the *Creating and using keywords* section in *Chapter 3, Advanced Configuration*, deploying keywords correctly is really important as they give us the means of creating connections between various services on various hosts, and are thus ideally suited for a high-level view of our IT estate.

Filters are again available in most dashlets to remove unwanted information, so use them as required.

The Process Map dashlet

Although process maps are considered a business dashlet, they also offer great possibilities to a technical team.

The **Process Map** is a powerful aide in visualizing any complex system in an attractive manner while showing the required technical information.

We have already seen a simple example of a map but just to underline its power, here is another example of a more complex environment (you can make these maps as complex as you want).

In this case the map shows a three-tier application in which our customers connect to our outside firewall and are then sent to one of the two web servers. Our web servers connect to our inside firewall and then on to the application servers, which in turn uses our database servers.

The following map contains service indicators (the circles), host indicators (the squares), some keyword-based indicators (the stars), hostgroup indicators (the square with three boxes below it), and finally some metrics showing the traffic flowing through our application (the arrows).

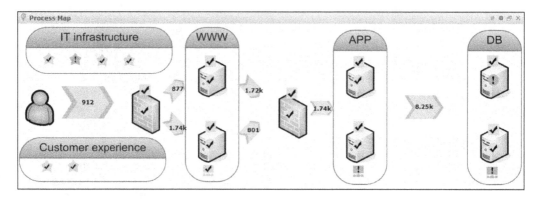

Each host has two indicators displaying its overall health (top) and application health (bottom), and both our database and application layers are experiencing issues with their applications; however, due to redundancy, our service has not been impacted.

We have applied two keywords to indicate our **Customer experience**, for instance, timing our website when performing certain actions such as ordering products.

Summary

In this final chapter we looked at one of Opsview's most eye-catching features and hopefully showed you the possibilities available to visualize your IT estate using dashboards.

Visualization can really help in not only viewing any issues, but also in terms of understanding how a system or application is built and what we need to monitor to make sure nothing is missed.

As Opsview keeps on developing new features and modules, the dashboards will keep on evolving too.

Index

K

keyword dashlets 122
keywords
  creating 30
  Keyword view setting, enabling 31, 32
  using 30

L

**Lightweight Directory Access Protocol
      (LDAP) 13**
Linux agent
  plugins, adding to 46
list_unknown_devices tool 65
Log4perl 68

M

main databases
  Opsview 97
  Runtime 97
Metric Pie Chart dashlet 124
monitoring 73
monitoring screen 26
**Monitoring | Status Detail | Network
      screen 40**
Monitors tab 20
MRTG 53
multi-homed environments 77
multi-master module
  about 109
  using 110
Multi Masters button 110
multiple Opsview Core systems
  deploying 72
Multi Router Traffic Grapher. *See* **MRTG**
multitenancy
  about 94
  tenancies, creating 94, 95

N

Nagios 15
NagVis 53
NAS (Network Attached Storage) 125
NetAudit module
  about 110

  enabling 111, 112
  RANCID, integrating 110
  using 111
NetFlow dashboard 128, 129
NetFlow module
  about 112
  configuring 113, 114
  NetFlow information, viewing 115
  tenancy 115
Network Analyzer module
  about 110
  NetAudit module 110-112
  NetFlow module 112-115
Network Management Information System.
      See **NMIS**
Network map dashlet 124
network outages 78
network scan
  starting 88
New Host page 17
New Primary Role option 95
New Service Check screen 21
nlcat tool 66
NMIS
  enabling 54
Note Pad dashlet 128
notifications
  configuring 34-36
  shared notification profiles 37
  shared notification profiles, using 37
  using 76
Notifications screen 13
Notifications tab
  about 35
  setting 36
Notify for settings 36
nProbe program 114
NRD (Nagios Result Distributor) 99
**NRPE: Command <my command> not
      defined 69**
NRPE (Nagios Remote Plugin Executor) 45
**NRPE: Return code of 127 is out of bounds -
      plugin may be missing 69**
**NRPE: Return code of 255 is out of bounds
      error 70**
NSCA interface 24

Thank you for buying
Monitoring with Opsview

About Packt Publishing

Packt, pronounced 'packed', published its first book "*Mastering phpMyAdmin for Effective MySQL Management*" in April 2004 and subsequently continued to specialize in publishing highly focused books on specific technologies and solutions.

Our books and publications share the experiences of your fellow IT professionals in adapting and customizing today's systems, applications, and frameworks. Our solution based books give you the knowledge and power to customize the software and technologies you're using to get the job done. Packt books are more specific and less general than the IT books you have seen in the past. Our unique business model allows us to bring you more focused information, giving you more of what you need to know, and less of what you don't.

Packt is a modern, yet unique publishing company, which focuses on producing quality, cutting-edge books for communities of developers, administrators, and newbies alike. For more information, please visit our website: www.packtpub.com.

About Packt Open Source

In 2010, Packt launched two new brands, Packt Open Source and Packt Enterprise, in order to continue its focus on specialization. This book is part of the Packt Open Source brand, home to books published on software built around Open Source licenses, and offering information to anybody from advanced developers to budding web designers. The Open Source brand also runs Packt's Open Source Royalty Scheme, by which Packt gives a royalty to each Open Source project about whose software a book is sold.

Writing for Packt

We welcome all inquiries from people who are interested in authoring. Book proposals should be sent to author@packtpub.com. If your book idea is still at an early stage and you would like to discuss it first before writing a formal book proposal, contact us; one of our commissioning editors will get in touch with you.

We're not just looking for published authors; if you have strong technical skills but no writing experience, our experienced editors can help you develop a writing career, or simply get some additional reward for your expertise.

open source *
community experience distilled

PUBLISHING

Administrating Solr

ISBN: 978-1-78328-325-5   Paperback: 120 pages

Master the use of Drupal and associated scripts
to administrate, monitor, and optimize Solr

1. Learn how to work with monitoring tools
   like OpsView, New Relic, and SPM

2. Utilize Solr scripts and Collection Distribution
   scripts to manage Solr

3. Employ search features like querying,
   categorizing, search based on location,
   and distributed search

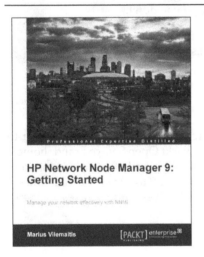

HP Network Node Manager 9: Getting Started

ISBN: 978-1-84968-084-4   Paperback: 584 pages

Manage your network effectively with NNMi

1. Install, customize, and expand NNMi
   functionality by developing custom features

2. Integrate NNMi with other management
   tools, such as HP SW Operations Manager,
   Network Automation, Cisco Works, Business
   Availability center, UCMDB, and many others

3. Navigate between incidents and maps
   to reduce troubleshooting time

Please check **www.PacktPub.com** for information on our titles

www.ingramcontent.com/pod-product-compliance
Lightning Source LLC
Chambersburg PA
CBHW082119070326
40690CB00049B/3978

9 781783 284733